THE FORGOTTEN ART OF GROWING, GARDENING
AND COOKING WITH HERBS

FRONTISPIECE

Typical of the early 19th Century keeping room where the author and his family live in southern New Hampshire is the six-foot wide fireplace and granite hearthstone. Herbs, flowers, and a string of corn suspended from the beamed ceiling show an effective way of preserving the harvest for winter use. To the right, the author has vented a soapstone stove through the Dutch oven. This serves as a seasonal method of providing additional heat on damp days when herbs like parsley and dill are dried on screens above the stove.

The Forgotten Art of Growing, Gardening and Cooking with Herbs

By RICHARD M. BACON

Instructions and Recipes
for
Herb Planting, Growing, Harvesting, and Drying
and for
Gardening, Housekeeping, Decorating, Dyeing,
Cooking, and Eating with Herbs

PUBLISHED MCMLXXII BY

YANKEE INC.

DUBLIN, NEW HAMPSHIRE

This Book Has Been Prepared by The Staff of
YANKEE, INC.
edited by
Clarissa M. Silitch
designed by
Walter E. Richardson
•

diagrams by
Margo Letourneau

DEDICATION

NEALE

without whom
neither this book nor this life
would be possible

and

to those countless other herbalists
— living and dead —
to whom we are indebted for
inspiration and knowledge

5th Printing
———

FIRST EDITION

Copyright 1972, by Yankee, Inc.

Library of Congress Catalog Card No. 72-91864
ISBN 0-911658-51-3

CONTENTS

INTRODUCTION

In planning what to bring to an alien world, the earliest settlers on the New England coast based their decision on practicality. To sustain their faith the colonists brought their Bibles; to sustain life they brought enthusiasm, knowledge, a few possessions, and seeds.

It was the seeds and roots of the utilitarian herb, packed among their meager belongings, which were to be as carefully tended as their religion and flourish in the rich soil of the New World. These plants would feed and nourish the body. They would also provide the principal ingredients for the simples, beverages, dyes, pesticides, and fragrances necessary to function during the long, harsh winters.

In addition to the centuries of oral folklore about the properties and uses of herbs, some colonists brought hand-copied Still Room books that contained family information handed down from mother to daughter giving advice pertinent to running the household. The more learned owned copies of printed herbals which had first been published in the late fifteenth century and continued to be amended and reprinted thereafter.

These early herbals were largely concerned with theory and often confused with astrology and mysticism. The English herbalists lifted information freely from classical herb writers of Greece and Rome. Gerard, Culpepper, and Parkinson stand out as giants of purloined and elaborated information often indiscriminately mixed with acute botanical observation. German and French

herbals contained discussions of plant virtues that had been hoarded by the monks during the barbaric days of the Middle Ages; Spanish writers drew also from the lore of the Middle East and India.

On their arrival some of the plant life which greeted the colonists was familiar; a few native herbs — bee-balm and bloodroot — were introduced to them by the Indians; a great amount was sent back to Europe both for the sake of novelty and to be studied as potentially profitable exports. This was one of the earliest natural resources to be exploited in the New World to help defray the costs of colonization.

One of the first actions taken by the settlers was the planting of herbs for the necessary fresh food needed to restore health after a long sea voyage and a limited diet. The need for salad material was especially important. It was Capt. John Smith who planted his "little garden for sallets" on the coast of Maine and returned to it between voyages of discovery to harvest his crop. "Sallets" accompanied every meal. If eaten raw, there was some concern they would produce a melancholy spirit; therefore, prior to the seventeenth century in England, salads were cooked and prepared with a vinegar and oil dressing. In fact, much of the early settler's food — parsley, skirret, sorrel, and Good King Henry — which we know as herbs today was pickled or boiled and served either hot or cold.

In the European tradition the kitchen garden was the domain of the housewife. Because a garden presupposes a defined area in which a sense of order is imposed on Nature, the settler's garden generally flanked the house and was fenced against the intrusion of wild and domestic animals. Beyond the sight of casual visitor, the colonial housewife arranged her practical plantings. Usually the perennials went in one area, the annuals in another; deep-rooted herbs together, those with shallow roots somewhere else. Heights, textures, and combinations of foliage were of little concern at a time when practicality came first.

Principally her design of raised rectangular or square beds, cut by cross-walks and alleys to assure maintenance, allowed the housewife to mass plantings that could go undisturbed from year to year, to set out some that could be harvested all at once, and to provide room for a succession of plantings. Whatever the arrangement, it tested her ability to find what she needed at a particular time and to grow a great concentration of plant material in a limited area.

Occasionally some plants were included for sentiment to remind the settler of home, others were trans-

INTRODUCTION

planted from nearby woods if their usefulness had been proven. But the kitchen garden also contained pot herbs, onions, carrots, and members of the cabbage family. It was often unsightly during the growing season; gaps were apparent after harvesting and before new plants were established. Sometimes the wash was spread on the herbs to dry and absorb their fragrances before being packed away in chests. In an era not so far removed from ours in time as in progress, aesthetics gave way to utility.

It was not until a certain affluence and leisure crept slowly into their lives that the colonists planted a pleasure garden, usually under the principal windows of the homestead. This separation of functions came after the Renaissance and only recently is it being questioned in America as we learn more about the interrelationships of plant life. The pleasure garden consisted of bright blooming flowers that were showy but whose usefulness was no longer current. By the early nineteenth century rural and village houses were buffeted from the road by pleasure gardens that were traversed only by guests, adults, and well-behaved children on special occasions.

Many of the herbs the settler brought with him have since escaped to live in the wild — plants like yarrow, boneset, teasle, bouncing bet, chicory, and heal-all — so today we see such an abundance of blooms along the roadsides we think of them as wild flowers that have always been part of our landscape. Other herbs fell from grace when their usefulness either diminished or was forgotten and were gradually transplanted to the pleasure garden: peony, lily of the valley, foxglove, viola, iris, poppy.

Early records and seed lists provide evidence as to what the colonists considered essential herbs. Angelica, basil, burnet, dill, fennel, hyssop, marjoram, parsley, rosemary, savory, thyme, and tansy are just a few of the seeds John Winthrope, Jr., ordered from England in 1631. They show how little our standards and tastes have changed in the intervening centuries.

* * *

This book is designed to stimulate an interest in how to grow and use herbs in modern, practical ways. It is a primer for those with little or no experience and should help to pierce the folklore and mystique that has been allowed — in this country especially — to surround the functions of these homely and ancient plants.

It is further intended as an aid to the city dweller who can learn to cultivate plants on the window sill, fire escape or in the backyard, or to anyone who is already growing herbs but has not yet discovered their many uses and combinations.

Written on a New Hampshire farm, this book is largely concerned with herbs that can be grown successfully in the New England climate.

Several revivals of interest in herbs have occurred in this century, particularly during and just after periods of war when imports were curtailed and home food production became a national commitment. But because of our increasing concern for health and environment, today's interest seems more likely to last. With more leisure to fill, with questions about the safety of commercial additives in our food, with the sameness of pre-packaged efficiency meals and high prices, Americans are turning more and more to creative cooking with natural foods.

A division of herbs into what one considers essential for the beginner is a tenuous and personal thing. The choice here is based on experience and taste and on the premise that most of us are first captured by the possibilities of herbs in cooking, expand our interest to include herbal by-products, and finally increase our plantings both for aesthetic pleasure and for the historical associations these humble plants can provide.

This knowledge of how to grow and use herbs may lead the reader to pursue broader interests as well. It may make him question his daily fare, pursue simple, less sophisticated pleasures, and ultimately change his lifestyle.

In part, then, this book is a simple testimonial to leading a fuller life.

QUAKER HILL FARM – 1972

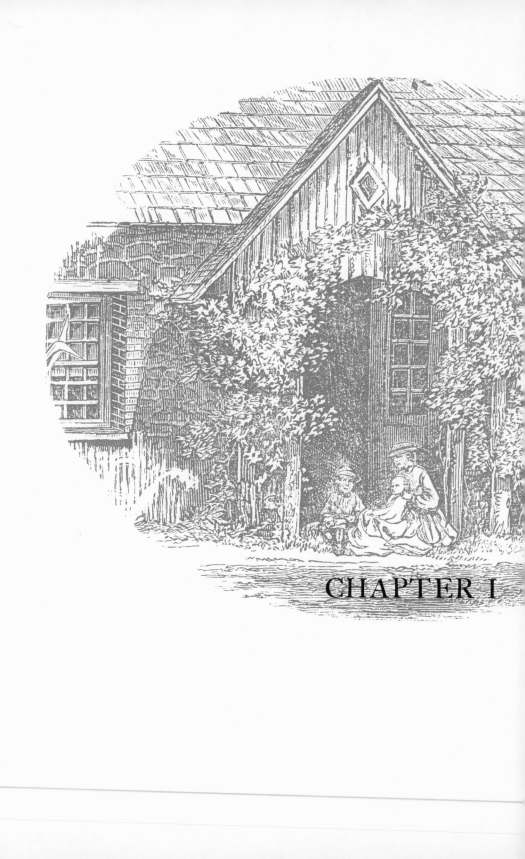

CHAPTER I

A Handful of Kitchen Herbs

Chives .... Parsley .... Basil .... Marjoram
.... Thyme .... Mint .... Lemon balm ....
Savory .... Sage .... Dill — seed and
weed .... Tarragon .... Rosemary .... Bay ....

A HANDFUL OF KITCHEN HERBS

CHAPTER I

Once you have tasted fresh herbs or those you have dried yourself, you will be convinced of their superiority over the packaged variety. We have found the following handful of kitchen herbs a good group for beginners to experiment with, because each can be easily grown in a limited space and offers a wide range of uses.

Chives

Always spoken of in the plural, chives are perennials which like well-drained, enriched soils to maintain robust plants and flavorful, hollow foliage. They are adaptable to either pots or the freedom of the garden. Outdoors, they will make an attractive border planting about 12 inches high and will develop feathery, purple blossoms. Although chives can be started from seed, they are so readily available in the spring at many food stores you would do well to buy a couple of pots and increase your planting either by separating the bulblets (with your fingers or a trowel, divide the scallion-like roots into smaller sections) and resetting them every few years or by allowing them to go to seed in the fall. By spring you will find they have self-sown profusely if grown outdoors.

To winter chives in the house, pot them in late summer and allow the foliage to die back and freeze for several weeks in the fall; they need this dormant period to stimulate growth for another season. In harvesting fresh chives, cut several stems low to the ground rather than trim only the tops of many; otherwise, the plant will become fragile and grasslike as it gradually loses its strong taste. This herb will slightly change the taste and appearance of food without leaving an aftertaste. Chives can be snipped over new boiled potatoes or used with meats, salads, and vegetables; they are a happy complement to cottage cheese and eggs. Choicest are the white-flowering garlic chives; they are less common and add a hint of garlic to food. Broad-leafed chives are a third variety which looks more robust than either of the others, but the flat leaves must be snipped more minutely.

Parsley

Green and fresh-looking, parsley is today used primarily as a garnish to provide a spot of color; having made its stylish appearance on the platter, it is often shoved aside like a stepchild by guests and children alike. A pity — this humble, slow-germinating biennial is more packed with vitamins, especially A and C — than almost any other common plant, Most classic seasonings require parsley, varying from a pinch to a cupful. Several varieties of seed are on the market. Broad-leafed Italian parsley is perhaps the best choice for the home gardener; its taste is stronger, it requires less washing, and it can be dried more easily. Curly parsley, however, makes a handsomer garnish.

Because parsley is a biennial, plantings should be made each year to insure a continuous supply. Plant the seed where you want this herb to grow — its long taproot resents disturbance — and be prepared for a long wait while it germinates. Pot a few plants early in the summer if you intend to bring them in the house later on.

Basil

Basil is a passport to Paradise in India, and one of its forms is considered sacred by the Hindus. In the western world, however, tradition tells us that to secure the best results we should curse and stamp upon the seeds as we sow them. Whichever way you regard it, this kingly plant always adds a spicy taste to dishes that contain tomatoes and has long been an essential ingredient of Italian cooking.

An annual, basil germinates quickly and dependably, and does not mind relocation once its second pair of true leaves develops. If allowed to blossom, it will perfume the air and attract honey bees. To have bushier plants and more foliage, however, snip off the bud stalk as it forms and leave about 12 inches between plants in either full sun or partial shade. Both green and purple varieties are useful in the kitchen, although the former is more popular. This herb is a tender annual and one of the first to be affected by the advent of cold weather.

Marjoram

Marjoram was adored by the ancients for its perfume-like taste. You'll find it delicious with squash or in veal dishes, breads, and salads. It can also be mixed with mints in hot teas. Wherever marjoram is used, it should be with discretion, for its odor and flavor are pervasive. Sweet marjoram, the kind most generally grown for the cook, is an annual in the north.

In the best seasons this dainty, somewhat finicky plant will grow less than 12 inches tall. When potted and brought indoors, it will turn a lighter green. One of the most attractive herbal house plants, marjoram will cascade in swirls over the rim of the container. Wild marjoram, a hardy perennial, is less aromatic and more sprawling in outdoor habit. This is a bee plant, easy to propagate by dividing the roots with a spade or trowel and replanting them 12 inches apart. The large purple flower heads are fine for winter bouquets, but we have found the flavor of the leaves becomes more subtle and less marjoram-like each year. Wild marjoram seeds are often sold as oregano, but

A HANDFUL OF KITCHEN HERBS
Thyme
Lemon thyme
Mints

---

this should not be confused with the herb associated with Italian dishes and Mexican cooking.

Thyme

Thyme has been the subject of literature and myth for as long as man can remember. Always pronounced "time," this plant is so open to word play that it has been enshrined for generations on sundials and immortalized by Shakespeare in "A Midsummer Night's Dream." One of the features of every classic garden was a raised bed or bank of thyme, which was believed to be the home of fairies. But beware of the bank "where the wild thyme blows" — the bees will be there first. Thyme is used in the kitchen with meats, vegetables, *bouquets garnis,* and breads.

You may have difficulty selecting from the more than 40 varieties of thyme. The most useful is *Thymus vulgaris,* which has dark green foliage, small white blossoms, and grows to a height of 8 inches. This can be kept in trim as a miniature hedge or allowed to sprawl. By anchoring down stray branches and covering them with soil, propagation of this perennial is simple. Cut the new plant from the parent when roots have developed and transplant it. Thyme is somewhat erratic in germinating, but once the seedlings take hold they will grow quickly. Lemon thyme is another variety to include in your first herb planting. It lends a slightly citrus taste to tomato soup, fish, and cream of vegetable soups and can give relief from a cold or sore throat. Thymol, one of the essential oils extracted from this family of herbs, is still an important ingredient of commercial cough medicines. Thyme is so easily dried and retains its flavor so long when properly stored, it seems unlikely you will want to winter a plant indoors unless you are interested in starting an unusual topiary.

Mint

Mint has perhaps been too closely associated with sauces and jellies for lamb, and one of its varieties is over-used in American toothpaste, cigarettes, and chewing gum. Nevertheless, this herb can bring such freshness to teas, salads, fruits, and drinks that its inclusion in the kitchen garden or window-sill planting is almost essential.

Given moist conditions and some shade in any garden or windowbox, the presence of mint will more than repay the gardener and cook. Start off with orange mint, apple mint, or plain mint bought as plants. (White mint seeds will germinate, they often result in a hybrid plant that is not a true variety.) Mint frequently is the bane of gardeners who have tried too late to contain it. All mints spread

Fig. 1. Potted fresh herbs. From left to right: marjoram; rosemary topiary; thyme (front); opal basil (rear); chives (front); lemon balm (rear); orange mint; and sage (far right). Photo by Stephen T. Whitney.

A HANDFUL OF KITCHEN HERBS
Lemon balm
Savory
Sage

---

from the roots — some more than others — and can be contained effectively either by sinking a metal or wooden barrier about 6 inches into the soil around the planting or by restricting each variety to a large sunken clay pot. Because mint beds can quickly become overcrowded and are susceptible to rust, they should be replanted every few years, or if room and time are not available, sliced vertically with an edging tool to break up the inevitable gnarl of roots.

Lemon Balm

A member of the mint family with a four-sided stem and mint-like flavor, lemon balm is easily grown, germinates dependably, and will maintain itself for years. It is a friend to the cook and drink maker, a plant adored by bees and kind to the victims of their stings, useful fresh as a furniture polish, and a comfort to the harried as a hot tisane. Its yellow-green leaves contrast nicely with the surrounding herbs; it stays in place and can even be cut back when it gets too tall. Lemon balm gives a lift to fruit salad and to the home gardener.

Savory

The "bean herb" was considered to be one of the strongest flavors in the kitchen garden before the importation of Eastern spices. Tradition-

ally coupled with snap beans, both winter and summer savory add a smoky, somewhat musty flavor to hot or cold beans and lentil soup and often can be used interchangeably with thyme. There seems little need for the beginning herb gardener to include both forms of this herb in his basic garden. Summer savory (the annual) germinates more quickly and is less strongly flavored than the perennial winter savory. Summer savory can be started in flats and transplanted, or sown directly in the garden. Plants should be spaced about 10 inches apart. They grow about 18 inches tall and present a rather spindly appearance, all their branches and tiny leaves pointing upwards from a central stem. It would be wise to start winter savory, however, with a purchased plant. This is an evergreen plant about 12 inches high, which can be harvested fresh all winter if provided with cover. Be sure to check the botanical name before buying seeds because some seedsmen may sell one variety for the other. Today we follow tradition by planting beans and savory in adjacent rows in the vegetable garden because these companionable plants interact to enhance the flavor of the beans and keep insect pests at a distance.

Sage

Sage, the familiar seasoning of

poultry stuffing and pork sausage, is otherwise neglected by most cooks today. Its dwindling reputation belies the days of glory this herb has seen. Believed by the ancient Greeks to be a cure-all, sage also played a significant role in early American history when it became the local tea substitute during the embargo. Later it was a highly desirable item to Chinese traders, who would barter four units of China tea for one of sage. Of unmistakable aroma, the leaves of common sage are thin and oval, with a pebbly texture. Their purple blossoms are pretty, if not spectacular, rising in spikes above the greenish-gray foliage. Several other varieties exist, but it is the hardy perennial common sage that is used by the cook.

Although sage germinates quickly and even young plants put forth abundant growth, they should be replaced every third year because they tend to develop woody, gnarled stems and fewer leaves as they become older. Sage can be used either fresh or dried. The fresh leaves have a more subtle taste; a little of the dried goes a long way. Today we use this herb to cut the richness of pork, goose, and wild game as well as to enhance the flavor of breads and cheeses. It has the digestive virtues of mint and can be used for sage tea or candied and served as a confection after dinner.

Dill

Dill and pickles have been coupled for at least 400 years. As good as dill pickles are, it is regrettable that this multipurpose herb should have so limited a reputation. Dill provides two products, seed and weed (a confusing label for the pungent, feathery leaves). The seed heads are thrown into the brine to make pickles or can be dried and separated from the stem to add to cookies or tomato soup; but the weed seems more versatile. It can be used with fresh tomatoes and cucumbers, fish, lamb stew, salads, home baked breads, and in recipes calling for sour cream. As a hot tea, dill has a slightly soporific effect. Plant dill where you want it to grow — but preferably not in the forefront of your garden, for it will reach a height of 2½ to 3 feet — or sow a few seeds in a pot at any time of year for indoor use, where it will not grow to such unmanageable proportions. If part of your outdoor planting is to produce seed heads about the time the cucumber crop is ready, thin the plants to stand about 8 inches apart and use the fresh thinnings or dry them for winter use. In the remainder of your planting clip off and use the weed before the plants reach a height of 12 inches, because once the stem develops, the weed will become sparse. Traditionally, dill seed has been used in an infusion to treat colic in children; it

A HANDFUL OF KITCHEN HERBS

Tarragon
Rosemary

---

was also respected for its ability to frighten away witches!

Tarragon

Tarragon, like bitter wormwood, is an artemisia. While not a spectacular plant, it is one of the most sought-after culinary herbs. Perhaps its fame rests most securely on the widespread use of tarragon vinegar, but it is also used in classic French sauces. Its fresh leaves add a hint of anise to salad, fish, poultry, eggs, and vegetables. This herb *can* be dried, but the process often makes the leaves brown and unattractive, and their taste sweeter. When ready to establish this perennial either outdoors or as a houseplant, be aware that French tarragon — the variety widely used by cooks — does not produce seed. When tarragon seed is advertised, it is the inferior Russian variety. So start with a French tarragon plant. This can be propagated by separating the clump in the early spring when the first new growth appears. Do this by lifting the plant with a spade, pulling the base of the stems outwards with your thumbs, and working down gently to release the gnarl of roots. Plant each rooted stem, allowing enough room for development and cultivation. Normally tarragon will reach a height of about 2½ feet outdoors and needs to be kept free from weeds and planted in a well-drained site in full sun. If the twisted, interwoven root growth of tarragon is allowed to become waterlogged, the plant will quickly die.

Rosemary

Of all the plants in this handful of essential kitchen herbs, the noble rosemary is the one that will bear the most careful watching — especially when grown indoors — yet somehow provides the greatest satisfaction, with its piny-fragrance and regal appearance. Historically, rosemary was used at weddings and gilded to decorate both home and church at Christmas. It is the herb of remembrance and was thrown into open graves or presented to a friend. It is believed that where rosemary thrives, the woman is dominant. Rosemary adds freshness to fowl, meats, breads, or citrus fruits. It can even be mixed with pipe tobacco or other herbs for a special kind of woodsy, outdoor aroma.

It is a tender perennial in the north and must be brought into the house as cold weather approaches. Although this herb is said to germinate slowly and uncertainly, we have been rewarded with seedlings in a February flat in ten days. Its development is almost painfully slow during the first year, so do not expect to be able to harvest many leaves for some time. Either in the summer garden or in the house, rosemary is easy to train as a topiary (see Chapter IV), but reacts quickly to neglect and should be sprayed with a fine mist to keep its needle-like leaves green and fresh. Drying out is as bad for its roots as letting them have too much water; either will quickly kill the plant.

Bay

Finally, sweet bay is an indispensable herb that should be treated much the same as rosemary in the New England climate. Planted in a tub and kept in a cool part of the house in the winter, this tender perennial can grow to a height of 3 - 6 feet. In summer, sink the tub in the garden to provide an interesting focal point. The pungent leaves are versatile but should be used with discretion. They are cooked with soups and stews, incorporated in *bouquets garnis,* rubbed on steaks before cooking, and added to the bath.

CHAPTER II

Some Herbs
Often Overlooked

Chervil ... Angelica ... Lovage ... Garlic and shallots ... Borage ...
Sweet cicely ... Woodruff ... Coriander ... Anise ... Caraway ... Fennel
... Calendula ... Camomile ... Beebalm ... Comfrey ... *et al.*

SOME HERBS OFTEN OVERLOOKED

CHAPTER II

After you have experimented successfully with the herbs discussed in the previous chapter, try your hand at some herbs less commonly grown, or neglected because of ignorance of their merits, lack of space, or changing fashion.

Chervil

Chervil is short, dainty, and parsley-like — one of the traditional French *fines herbes*. This almost makes it an essential herb for the cook, but most agree that its slight anise taste is effective only in conjunction with other herbs. Excellent in omelettes, cold summertime soups (like consommé and cucumber), and salads, it can also be infused in vinegar or frozen in small amounts to give winter egg dishes a lift.

Though not a robust plant, chervil will thrive, given a shady spot in a pot or in the garden under the protection of some lusher, taller herb. Often it self-sows freely, once established, so a single planting should last several years. Like lettuce, chervil can be sown at intervals to assure a steady supply.

Angelica

Angelica has the reputation of possessing heavenly qualities and in medieval days was used to ward off the plague. The hollow stems can be added to rhubarb and fruit dishes or cut into small pieces and candied to use as a confection or cake decoration. The leaves, either dried or fresh, can be made into a soothing herbal tea.

Angelica is a tall biennial which you can start from fresh seed. It needs a shady back border and does well in moist soil, even on the north side of the house. When you grow angelica, leave room for mass planting. It will pay to let some of the seed heads mature and self-sow for the following year.

Lovage

Lovage is gigantic, coarse, and strong-tasting. It imparts to soups, stews, and salads a sharp celery-like taste, and should be used with a light touch. Not for the gardener with limited space, this perennial can tower up to 6 feet in the first season, which may account for its diminished popularity. Put it in the back of the garden, because lovage will dominate the landscape. It will grow untended once established and is easy to propagate by division. Lovage leaves dry well but tend to blanch quickly when exposed to sunlight. Keep it from flowering by cutting off the flower stalks before they develop, and growth will be directed to producing larger leaves and stems.

Garlic and Shallots

Many beginning herb growers think of garlic and shallots as com-

Chervil, angelica
Lovage, garlic, shallots
Borage, salad burnet
Sweet cicely, woodruff

mon vegetables, yet they are indeed herbs, indispensable to good cooking and health, and repellent to insects and animal pests. They will multiply quietly, with just an occasional weeding. You can purchase sets from seed houses or divide and plant the cloves of those you buy at the food store. In the New England climate, they will winter well in the garden and come up again in the spring, ready for another season.

There are four early spring herbs you may want to consider for your garden because they are ready for use before many other plants have matured.

Borage

Borage is a showy herb noted for the intensity of its blue blossoms. Its lush, hairy leaves, unless trimmed occasionally, will soon cause it to resemble an outrageously overfed African violet. Because this annual seeds itself freely in dry places, a single planting one year will last for many. The seedlings, however, will not observe the boundaries you may have intended, so transplant them when young. The tender leaves add the taste of cucumber to salad, and the blossoms are good to float on cooling drinks, to candy as confections, or to decorate a frosted cake.

Salad Burnet

Salad burnet is another early sea-son herb whose leaves can be added to salads, drinks, and vinegar infusions. This is a pretty perennial with round tooth-leafed foliage; it germinates quickly and will become a permanent member of the garden without maintenance problems.

Sweet Cicely

The name sweet cicely is enough to invoke the Elizabethan period, although this herb was used for food and medicine since before the time of the Greeks. Exceedingly easy to grow, it is an aesthetically rewarding plant, with lacy foliage and showy white blossoms, which are among the first to assert the coming of spring. Cicely seeds, long and nearly black when ripe, can be brought into the house for winter bouquets or used in the green stage to sweeten fruits. The young leaves of this perennial are added to early spring salad, and the roots can be boiled and eaten as a vegetable.

Woodruff

Woodruff is a woodsy, shade-loving groundcover that multiplies readily from the roots when provided with damp conditions; it is best to plant this perennial in a humus soil beneath a garden tree or under shrubs. It is used primarily to flavor May wine (float the blossoms in it), but it will not flower in New Hampshire in time for the May Day cele-

SOME HERBS OFTEN OVERLOOKED

Coriander
Anise, caraway
Fennel

---

bration unless brought into the greenhouse and forced. When dry, woodruff exudes the scent of fresh-cut hay and has traditionally been used as a strewing herb.

Another group of herbs to become acquainted with after your initial successes in garden and kitchen are those we depend on largely for their seeds: coriander, anise, caraway and fennel. These are not especially attractive plants and can be sown in rows in some untraveled spot, occasionally weeded, and neglected during the summer. Their harvest is covered in Chapter V.

Coriander

Coriander is one of the few growing herbs I find repugnant. Its name is said to mean "having a buglike odor," which may account for my personal prejudice. But I grudgingly put up with its muskiness while weeding because, when dried, the round seeds take on a surprising sweetness that adds enormously to the taste of baked apples and pies, breads, and baked potatoes. Coriander leaves are used in preparing Chinese, Mexican, and Eastern dishes; Orientals believe the seeds help ensure immortality.

Anise

Anise provides a flavor fairly common among herbs in seed form. The basis of some liqueurs, the seeds were used by the colonists as well as the Romans to aid digestion. Sow this annual early; the crop needs a long season to mature.

Caraway

The only biennial among these seed herbs, caraway is associated with cookies, dark breads, and cheeses. The strong taste is distinctive and favored by many. Growing to a height of 2 feet, this herb is credited with the power to keep lovers true and to cure hysterics — which properties may or may not be related.

Fennel

The seed is used in cookies and tea, or administered to children with colic. The plant resembles dill but has a bulbous growth at the base of the stem. If you do not grow fennel for its seed, use the stalks for a winter vegetable, as the Italians do, or serve them in a marinade in hot weather. Popular since before Biblical times, the feathery fennel weed has long been coupled with fish cookery. In the sixteenth century this was a common strewing herb that infused the air with its slight anise scent and rid the house of fleas and witches.

Calendula

The showy open blossoms — or-

Fig. 2. Hanging fresh herbs. From left to right: southernwood; apple mint (above); *green bush basil* (below); *sage* (above); *marjoram* (below); *and fennel in the seed stage.* Photo by Stephen T. Whitney.

SOME HERBS OFTEN OVERLOOKED

Calendula
Camomile
Beebalm, comfrey

---

ange, red, or yellow — of calendula add late-season color to garden or window plantings. Historically known as pot marigold, this annual was used in early Saxon times for a variety of medical complaints and still colors food as a poor man's substitute for the expensive imported saffron. Calendula germinates easily in early flats or directly in the garden. Petals from its sun-loving blossoms can be added to fresh salad and soups and form the basis for several of the herbal by-products mentioned in Chapter VIII.

Herbs which make, fresh or dried, aromatic and healthful teas (see Chapter VI), should also be included in your garden. Beside the mints, four basic tea herbs are camomile, beebalm, comfrey, and catnip.

Camomile

A hardy perennial, camomile gained a lasting reputation when administered to Peter Rabbit, whose mother must have been drawing on her knowledge of folklore. Camomile flowers have been used as a home remedy since early Egyptian times. By the middle of the sixteenth century, this herb was known to induce perspiration. Tea made from camomile is soothing, smells slightly of apples, and is today a popular herbal beverage. Creeping forms were

planted as lawns in Europe long before the invention of mechanical grass cutters. The small, daisy-like flowers are harvested and dried when the white petals begin to turn back.

Beebalm

One of the few native American herbs, beebalm was introduced to the colonists by the American Indian. It has been known also as Oswego tea, bergamot, fragrant balm, red balm, and Indian's plume. All species are hardy perennials and can be propagated either from seed or root division. The most striking is *Monarda didyma,* with brilliant scarlet flowers. Beebalm also comes in white and varying shades of magenta. A member of the mint family, it prefers partial shade and moist soil, and grows to a height of about 2 feet.

Comfrey

For years this vigorous perennial herb was used to help knit broken bones and as a tea to treat lung troubles. Today comfrey is regaining popularity among natural-food enthusiasts as a tea. Its medicinal properties are discussed on page 63 ff.

Catnip

Catnip often grows rank and untended near old farm buildings. It has teased generations of cats, but I am ready to lead a crusade to take this delightful and healthy plant away from them and put it back on the pantry shelf. Catnip makes a pleasing winter tea that encourages restful sleep and is used to combat incipient colds and fevers. A persistent, hardy plant, catnip can be started from seed or divided. It was brought to America by 1620 as a household remedy and has become naturalized in many areas.

In further expansion of your herb garden you will eventually want to cultivate some of the herbs that helped form the literature and folklore of our civilization. These would include lavender and rue, santolina, hyssop, germander, yarrow, pennyroyal, tansy, and three of the artemisias.

Lavender

Sweet-scented lavender, one of the most consistently popular herbs in history, still holds its own as the basis of many herb products despite competition from synthetic perfumes. Of the several varieties, *Lavandula vera* is the one to start with. Seeds are slow to germinate, but plants are readily available at nurseries. Although lavender does not grow as tall here as it does in England and California, it will soon broaden and reward you with long spikes of purple blossoms that can be dried for use in sachets or teas or extracted for toiletries.

Rue

Rue, the Herb of Grace, is more important today for its appearance than for its utility, although rue leaves can be included in a green salad. Its bluish-green foliage, unique among plants, its yellow button flowers, and erect graceful stance lend a distinguished accent to a herb planting. Long used as an insecticide and strewing herb, rue is said to ward off pestilence and fever. Some have to be wary of this plant, which if brushed just before flowering, has been known to cause welts similar to those caused by poison ivy. Easy to germinate, rue is sometimes killed by northern winters but generally comes through year after year.

Santolina and Hyssop

These herbs are decorative, and if kept trim, both will make fine miniature hedges to separate plantings. Purchase healthy grey or green santolina plants and propagate by root divisions. In the north, provide winter cover; snow weight and frost heaves threaten this perennial. Santolina is used as a moth repellent.

Hyssop is recommended for its longevity, for its role as a traditional bee plant, and for its use as an antidote for the stings of bees and

SOME HERBS OFTEN OVERLOOKED
Germander
Yarrow
Pennyroyal, tansy

wasps. It is easily grown from seed in purple, white, or pink blossoming varieties, the first being the most common.

Germander

Another decorative perennial herb, germander also makes a handsome miniature hedge in climates too cold for boxwood. It has dark, glossy foliage and should be purchased as a plant.

Yarrow

Yarrow is said to have been used by Achilles to staunch the flow of blood among his soldiers at the Battle of Troy. It is a perennial which grows in a clump to a height of 3 feet and can be either divided or started handily from seed. The golden variety is the most robust and will reward the herb grower with both its insecticidal properties and its closely packed umbrels of showy blossoms, wonderful for winter bouquets. Now naturalized, yarrow is often regarded as a native wild flower.

Pennyroyal

Another member of the mint family, pennyroyal is an annual that reseeds freely once a planting has been established. Of low, creeping growth, this is a good herb to use at the edge of a raised bed where it will cascade to break the hard visual lines. It has a pungent odor and is used as a tea and as a repellent for fleas and black flies.

Tansy

Tansy, planted near the doorstep, is said to discourage flies from entering the house. Rarely used today either in cooking or as a tea, this bitter perennial has pesticidal properties. It grows about 3 feet tall and in late summer is crowned with yellow button blossoms that are dried for winter bouquets. A single plant will spread rapidly from the roots and will have to be kept constantly in place. Until fairly recently, tansy was used as a spring tonic, and because of its acrid, somewhat medicinal scent, was laid in the coffin during home burials to mask unpleasant odors.

With the exception of tarragon, the artemisias have been excluded from modern cooking. But if you desire muted greens and grays in your herb garden, you will want some representatives of this family — wormwood, southernwood, and silver mound, for a start.

Wormwood

Wormwood is the bitter herb of Biblical times. Formerly used as the basis of absinthe, it is still employed as a worming medicine for farm animals and as an ingredient of many liqueurs, vermouth, and liniments. Usually slow to germinate, it will nevertheless reward your patience as a durable foundation plant that will combat insects in the garden. Wormwood grows to a sprawling height of 3 feet. Its silvery gray foliage can be used in fresh or dried bouquets; in late summer insignificant yellow blossoms form along the tips of the stems. If it sprawls too much, this herb can be drastically cut back in midsummer.

Southernwood

About the same height as wormwood, southernwood is more feathery in appearance, with green, fine foliage. This perennial has a delicious scent and is used as a moth and insect repellent. Historically, it was known as lad's love, for southernwood was believed to promote the growth of a young man's beard if fresh leaves were rubbed on his cheeks.

Silver Mound

Silver mound has no modern use; we grow it purely for its appearance. Low and feathery, this artemisia forms a symmetrical clump of light gray foliage about 12 to 14 inches across that makes an unusual accent among the muted colors of the herb garden. Several nurseries advertise it under different names, but silver mound is easy to recognize from its appearance.

The herbs suggested in this and the preceding chapter are generally easy to obtain from herb nurseries and seedsmen (see Appendix C, p. 121).

CHAPTER III

A Time for
Making Plans

Plants or seeds? .... Planting—soil readiness, spading, sowing .... Thinning ....
Flats—indoor planting .... Transplanting—"pricking off," "hardening off,"
weather .... Arrangements—formal, old-fashioned, garden-plan diagrams

A TIME FOR MAKING PLANS

CHAPTER III

To prescribe one form [of garden] *for every man*
to follow were too great a presumption and folly;
for every man will please his owne fancie . . .

John Parkinson (1629),
Paradisi in Sole Paradisus Terrestris

Ideas for arranging your herb plot can be garnered from countless sources — old herbals, books, and magazines. Familiarize yourself with the plants and their growing habits by studying them at first hand in herb nurseries and in the many gardens maintained by herb societies and garden clubs at historic houses and arboretums. Indeed, half the pleasure in planning a herb garden is visiting nurserymen and finding new specimens for your collection. Though the gardener may "please his owne fancie" in selecting and placing his herbs, the site, amount of sunlight, and condition of the soil will determine the success or failure of his efforts. Planning — choosing the herbs to grow, estimating the numbers and kinds of plants required to provide the necessary supply of fresh and dried herb, and careful layout of the garden — is important in getting off to a good start with herbs.

Plants or Seeds

Whether to begin with plants or seeds is a major decision which will depend on your patience, your pocketbook, and the particular herb. Plants give quick results but are enormously expensive compared to seed. On the other hand, you probably cannot use all the plants that will germinate from the contents of a single seed packet. Thus, where you only require a half dozen plants of a certain variety or where you do not wish to go to the effort of raising plants from seed, it is better to purchase this variety as plants. In the case of a herb like French tarragon that does not produce seeds, a healthy plant is essential. Do not take the apparent short-cut of buying a packet of mixed seed. Even the experienced gardener will find it hard to identify the seedlings, and it is better to be sure than to be left in doubt for several seasons to come.

Some basic herbs are slow to germinate and almost grudging in their growth habits the first season. Perhaps your enthusiasm and finances will dictate your buying herbs such as rosemary and lavender as plants. Once you have them growing, they will be available for cuttings, and later, when time allows, you can start your own from seed.

Seeding

Some seeds remain viable for years; others must be planted as soon as the seeds ripen in the fall. In general, it is wiser to purchase new seeds each year and so avoid disappointment from seeds that fail to germinate. Most nationally known garden catalogs now feature a special herb section. For a wider range of seeds available, collect catalogs from nurseries that grow herbs exclusively (see Appendix C).

Before opening the first seed packet, recall the myth of parsley. The tradition is that parsley seed goes seven or nine times to the Devil and back again before it germinates. With each visit, Satan retains some for his own. So never expect complete germination, and be prepared to wait out the seemingly endless time it takes for the seeds to show signs of life.

The age of the seed, the moisture, temperature, and condition of the soil at seeding time will all affect the rate at which seeds germinate. Too much water will rot them; too little will dry them out. And because these conditions will vary from year to year, so will the germination process.

Be sure to study the planting directions on the packet. Some herbs must be started early in flats and provided with gentle bottom heat to overcome a short growing season and assure a respectable harvest. Other seeds must first be frozen before they will break dormancy, and certain large seeds must be nicked with a penknife to facilitate germination. Sort your seeds into categories depending on the growing instructions — this saves hours of frustration. If you do start seeds in flats, make sure that the flats are located where conditions favor growth — in a sunny window, a cold frame, or a greenhouse. If none of these locations is available, buy plant lamps (grolamps) to give artificial light from a garden-supply center and rig up a seedbed in the cellar, spare room, or corner of your living room.

If bumper crops and great variety are not your aim, seed herbs directly out-of-doors at the time recommended for your climate zone. To check the receptivity of the soil in spring, take a fistful of loam and compact it. Watch how the soil reacts as you open your hand. If there is no change in the compressed ball, it is better to wait; the moisture content is too high and will rot the seeds. Working the soil now may cause a hard crust to form later and prevent moisture from seeping down to the roots during the summer. If, however, it falls away slowly from the mass, the soil is ready, and the process of preparing the seedbed can begin.

A TIME FOR MAKING PLANS

Sowing
Thinning
Flats

Spade the ground deeply and rake the surface smooth. In seeding herbs out of doors, we have found that broadcasting in rectangular beds with the idea of thinning or transplanting when the plants are established is not conducive to happy gardening. This may be the procedure recommended for field crops like buckwheat and clover, but weeding emerging herbs can be a frustrating business. Garden soil is not sterile, but packed with all kinds of seeds just as receptive to good conditions as your herbs are. And weeds and herbs are great look-alikes!

Therefore, sow the herbs in rows. Label every row clearly and record your work in a garden journal. Else you may become impatient and dig up or tread down entire plantings that are merely engaged in germination. The records of planting dates and conditions you keep in the garden journal will prove invaluable in ensuing years. (See "Notes — A Gardener's Journal" at the back of this book.)

Thinning

When the second pair of true leaves has developed, it is time to thin. No plant enjoys being crowded; this fosters erratic growth and usually results in too much stem and too little leaf or seed development. Relieve congested plantings by removing the extras and leaving the remaining plants evenly spaced. Dispose of the extras or transplant them to another row or permanent bed.

Some herbs enjoy being coddled and transplanted. Basil, savory, marjoram, thyme, sage, and rosemary will react by bushing out as soon as they are given the chance. Deep-rooted herbs, however, may express resentment unless transplanted very early. Dill, parsley, and fennel should be left where they were planted and merely thinned. Treatment of a crop like dill depends on the use you plan for it. If you want dill weed for salads and drying, let a portion of the row alone and mulch it as the weather warms. If your aim is dill seed, thin the plants to stand about 12 inches apart. This will encourage them to develop seed heads by late summer — about the time you have a bumper crop of cucumbers.

Flats

To start plants in flats, any type of container will do — cut-down plastic milk jugs, cottage cheese cartons, even paper cups with a plastic coating — as long as drainage is provided and the starting medium is sterile and contains a good mixture of soil, sand, and vermiculite. Adding about one-third sand will lighten the medium and allow excess water

KEY:

Theme		Variation (for cold winters)	
☐	Green Santolina	☐	Roman Wormwood
■	Grey Santolina	▨	Hyssop
▨	Hyssop	■	Catmint *(Nepeta mussini)*
▨	Germander	▨	Lamb's Ears

● Topiary rosemary, Privet clipped, Bay, Bird Bath or Sundial

Fig. 3. Formal knot garden. The planting design and the colors of the herbs used create the optical illusion of a continuous line passing over and under itself. To preserve the illusion, the borders must *be kept exact by careful weeding and trimming. This example is 6' square, and can either be raised and bordered with bricks or boards, or set as the focal point in a larger formal pattern.*

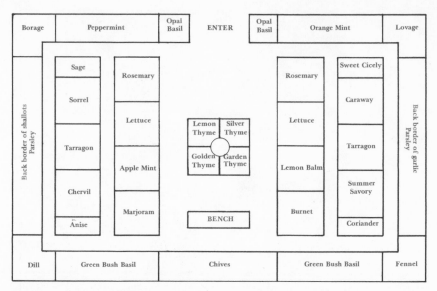

Fig. 4. Kitchen garden. An excellent plan that will provide a herb-loving cook with everything she needs. Easy to work in, and pretty, too.

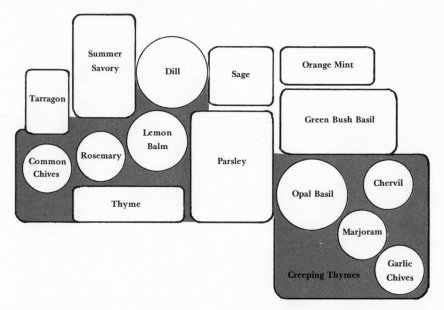

Fig. 5. Another kitchen garden, with herbs in pots and tiles of various heights. This can be "planted" on a terrace or patio by removing bricks or slate and sinking the containers in crushed gravel or marble chips. Plant shaded areas with creeping thymes. Leave space around this low-rise garden for watering and harvesting.

to run off before it rots the seedlings.

When you have sprinkled the seeds on the growing surface and either pressed them into the soil or covered them thinly, put ·glass, newspaper, or a plastic bag over the flat to retain the moisture. Glass and plastic should be lifted once a day and wiped dry to prevent the accumulation of excessive moisture which may encourage "damping off," a fungus disease that attacks emerging seedlings at soil level. If this does start, remove affected plants promptly. Should it become widespread, there is little you can do but begin again in sterile flats. Once germination is under way, remove the covering and expose the flats to increasing amounts of light.

Indoor seeding should be started about four to six weeks ahead of the time you would normally plant seeds in the garden. However, some perennials should be seeded as early as January to obtain good growth during the first season. The seedsman's directions should decide this. Sometimes you will find you have been too eager for spring and have large numbers of husky plants on hand long before you can set them out-of-doors. This is likely to result in woody stems and retarded growth later on unless you reduce the temperature and withhold fertilizer and moisture (but not so much

as to cause marked wilting). A good practice is not to plant all your seeds at once. Hold some back until you see how well you have done at normal planting time; another planting may be in order.

Leggy plants — those with weak, long stems — are the result of too little light. It is better to increase the amount of light so the plants will develop strong root systems while indoors. This will assure better adjustment to outdoor conditions when the time comes to set them in the garden. Rearrange the flats daily according to the light source, and growth will be more uniform (see Chapter IV).

Transplanting

"Pricking off" is the term used by horticulturists for the process of transplanting seedlings from the flat to new containers in order to achieve better spacing while still indoors. This can be done easily with a kitchen fork. As you loosen the soil, try to cause as little disturbance as possible to the root system. Handle the seedlings by their leaves rather than by their stems as you transplant them. Remember to inscribe new labels and mark the new plantings accurately. Today's neglect leads to tomorrow's confusion.

Before they can be established in the outdoor garden, tender plants

A TIME FOR MAKING PLANS

Transplanting
Arrangements
Placing herbs

must undergo a period of adjustment to the natural world. This is called "hardening off" and should be done whether you grow your own plants or buy them from a greenhouse. Flats should be increasingly exposed to outdoor temperatures during the day for several days and brought back into the house at night. The plants will readily become used to the harsher conditions of the outside world, and their stems will become tougher. A temporary cold frame will achieve better results and eliminate carrying back and forth if nighttime temperatures are not too low.

Transplanting to a permanent outdoor site should be done on an overcast day or during a gentle rain. Such weather gives plants time to adjust to their new location without sun burning their leaves or wind drying them.

Arrangements

Now is the time to please your "owne fancie." Resurrect your plans and dreams. To plan any kind of garden, formal or informal, do some homework with pencil, paper, and measuring tape. Take notes from publications and visits to other gardens. Lay out your design as a scale drawing.

A herb garden lends itself to tailored arrangements — beds of plants in geometric design, precise,

clipped borders (such as hyssop, germander, or thyme), weedless areas neatly mulched or graveled, and ample pathways giving room for both work and enjoyment. Locating a specific herb when needed is easier when the herbs are planted in blocks. Major walks are usually ordained by traffic patterns, while arterial paths will allow you to get from one bed to another conveniently. Straight lines, vistas, and focal points, trademark of the classical age, may be employed even on a diminutive scale to bestow a sense of order and well-being.

Some prefer the less formal, "old-fashioned," arrangement, where the plants grow cheek-by-jowl and development is largely unchecked. Others settle for the traditional colonial pattern of long, rectangular raised beds. Another possibility is to plant in beds of various geometric shapes; with this type of garden, plant so that the different beds with plants of varying size and height present an attractive prospect from both within and without the house.

If you are growing vegetables, herbs planted among or interspersed with them are reputed to have pesticidal properties (see Chapter IX). Take into account existing trees and shrubs in your garden plan. There dappled shade will add interest, give relief from summer heat, and encourage the growth of shade-loving

Fig. 6. Typical raised-bed herb garden. Note labeled sticks.

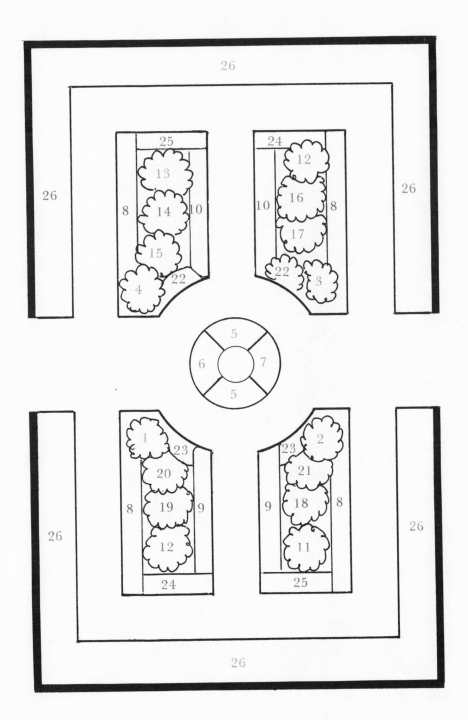

herbs such as woodruff, sweet cicely, beebalm, and European ginger. The mint family also appreciates shade, with moist soil.

When you have sketched in building locations, trees, and shrubs on your scale drawing, you are ready to place the herbs. Remember that while sunlight and drainage are the most essential factors to consider, convenient access is also important. (see pp. 35-36 and page 40 for diagrams of suggested plantings.) Perennials will be left permanently in their location; they can be divided about every three years or exchanged for a new plant when they become too woody and unpro-

ductive. Biennials must be left undisturbed for two years, and annuals are summer boarders.

Think of the future, then, as you plant your first herb garden, allowing plenty of room for growth. Your tendency may be to overplant when the seedlings are small at the beginning of the season; if so, you will be forced to thin and rearrange them before they are ready. Plants adjust differently, even in adjacent gardens, and their growth depends on the soil, amount of sunlight, and the care you give them. A well planned garden should please both your "owne fancie" and that of your herbs.

Fig. 7. Perennial garden (Left). *Use the "knot garden" as the center plot or follow the plan and sink a bay in a tub at the unmarked center. A sundial, bee skep, or bird bath also make interesting focal points. Key: 1—artemisia silver mound; 2—winter savory; 3—grey santolina; 4—green santolina; 5—ladies' mantle; 6—silver thyme; 7—golden thyme; 8—germander or Roman wormwood; 9—lemon thyme; 10—common thyme; 11—rue; 12—lavender; 13—sage; 14—artemisia silver king; 15—sweet cicely; 16—beebalm; 17—apple mint; 18—southernwood; 19—yarrow; 20—orange mint; 21—lemon balm; 22—chives; 23—garlic chives; 24—burnet; 25—catmint* (Nepeta mussini); *26—hyssop (clipped).*

W.T. RICHARDS DEL.

R. TELFER SC.

CHAPTER IV

Gardening in Restricted Areas— Indoors & Out

Light and temperature – plant lamps, watering,
humidity and heat ... Potting and planting –
containers and potting soil, when to plant ...
Aloe ... Bay ... Lemon verbena ... Rosemary ...
Topiary ... High-rise herbs – wind and grime

GARDENING IN RESTRICTED AREAS — INDOORS AND OUT
CHAPTER IV

Many culinary herbs can be raised successfully on the window sill or in a specially constructed indoor planting area. The proper degrees of light, heat, and humidity — the three essentials to good plant growth — can be manufactured even in a modern house or apartment as saturated as it is with dry, twenty-four-hour heat.

Most houses today suffer from too much heat and too little humidity. Lushly blooming geraniums, begonias, and potted herbs in the southern windows of drafty farmhouses or "unimproved" city houses always look so healthy partly because they are grown under conditions most moderns consider below the comfort zone. Before central heating, the simmering tea kettle and wood stove provided enough humidity and heat during the day but allowed temperatures to drop when the fire was banked for the night.

Actually the kitchen window sill, while convenient, is the poorest place to raise potted plants in today's home. Unless provided with excellent ventilation, kitchen temperatures fluctuate over too great a range, while grease and odors will clog the pores of the plants.

Today many kinds of prepackaged herb-seed planters are on the market. Like so many consumer-oriented products, they offer convenience and promise. However, purchasers are often disappointed with the results. Sometimes, indeed, the seed is not fresh enough to assure germination. Often, however, the principal cause of failure is that the would-be indoor gardener does not have conditions conducive to good plant growth and does not understand how to remedy it. If they germinate, the seedlings are occasionally drowned with kindness and concern and not given the amount of light and temperature they need to sustain growth. Unless you are willing to improve the plant environment indoors, you would do well to concentrate on dried herbs for winter use and thereby avoid frustration and expense.

Light and Temperature

If you do not have a window with a southern exposure and at least half a day of sunlight, you can garden under lights in your home. For years we maintained a respectable winter garden in a narrow pantry with a single north window by hanging fluorescent plant lights above the pantry shelves and sink. These could be adjusted as the plants grew; the room, while convenient to the kitchen, was separated from it, and the heating vent could be turned off. Humidity could be maintained at the desirable level by filling the sink with water and dropping a plastic sheet over both sink and plants.

Often you can locate a second-hand store that sells used fixtures reasonably. These come in varying lengths with or without reflectors. It is better to find some with reflectors, but if not you can make a shield to direct the light to the plants from galvinized tin, aluminum foil, or even cardboard. Commercial plant lights are sold under various trade names by garden centers and hardware stores and come in several lengths with enough selection to fit your fixture and planting area. Buy wide-spectrum plant lights. Although these will give a purplish cast to the surroundings and are sometimes hard on the eyes, your garden will appreciate them.

If you do not want to go to this trouble, seed houses and garden centers offer attractive and expensive indoor gardening arrangements that are easy to assemble. If you are imaginative, however, the homemade kind will be just as effective and certainly less expensive and more personal.

When plants become tall and spindly, it is a sure sign they are not getting enough light. Fluorescent tubes should be kept about 6 inches above the tops of the plants, but remember to rearrange them often, since those plants under the center of the span will benefit the most. A plastic curtain can be suspended to enclose your planting especially at night so cooler temperatures can be maintained.

No matter how well tended your plants are, expect some of the leaves to yellow and die. You should pick these off, not only to maintain the appearance but also to check possible development of decay organisms. Yellowing leaves mean you are watering either too much or too little. Do not be hasty in watering; experiment to correct the condition, and little by little as the plants respond you will gain the experience to correct the situation.

The ultimate, of course, in indoor gardening is to be able to control the number of hours of light automatically. This can be done by purchasing a timer that can be plugged into the fixture. It will considerably lessen the possibility of human error and allow the plants both to thrive under the light and to rest when the timer clicks off.

Potting and Planting

If you have manufactured the proper conditions, you can grow parsley and chives, basil, tarragon, and chervil; also marjoram, thyme, dill, sage, savory, and rosemary. There are many others, but they may take up too much room and time. Although they tend to become a host to white flies, a pot of nasturtiums will also be a satisfying novelty for winter salads.

These herbs can be potted in individual clay or plastic containers

GARDENING IN RESTRICTED AREAS—INDOORS AND OUT

Planting
Containers
Potting Soil

where light will reach them for at least half a day, or better yet, they can be set in a 3-inch-high metal tray that has been layered with pebbles or cut gravel and fitted to your specific measurements. Keep the water level in the tray at the height of the pebbles to assure good humidity.

Metal and plastic containers are available, but wood is still the best for retaining moisture. You can buy ready-made wooden boxes and tubs, or you can have a local lumber dealer cut pieces to your specifications. The deeper the planter, the more satisfying the results. But if you are going to have to bring the containers indoors to continue to garden in winter, remember that the weight of wet soil increases disproportionally. Several smaller wooden planters are perhaps better than a single larger one, using the same growing medium as for potted herbs indoors.

Rather than pot each plant individually, fill the planter to within 2 inches of its rim and set out a combination of herbs. Here are some that grow attractively together. In a planter 4 feet long by 10 inches wide set out 4 clumps of chives, 2 of marjoram, and 1 each of summer savory and tarragon. Space them out with some additions and duplications and sink a pot of mint up to its rim. This will help contain the mint roots and make it easier to judge the dampness of the soil. Or try a planter

of sweet basil, marjoram, parsley, sage, summer savory, rosemary, dill, and thyme, or a combination of sweet basil, marjoram, parsley, and garlic chives.

Window-box gardening indoors is another satisfactory solution. Plant all the herbs, arranged according to height, in a wooden or metal box, making sure to lay pebbles or broken crock along the bottom for drainage before you add the growing medium. The only disadvantage of this planting arrangement is that it will be cumbersome to move when adjustments must be made for the light source.

Mixtures for container plants should be lighter than garden soil. Mix about two parts loam with one part peat moss and one of perlite or vermiculite to help retain moisture but prevent compacting. Of course fertilizer will also have to be administered about every ten days as the plants grow.

If you already have an herb garden outdoors and deplore the coming of winter and the loss of your resources, start some seeds in midsummer so as to have small plants to bring in by fall. It is not a good idea to pot mature plants like basil, parsley, and sage late in the season expecting them to thrive in confinement. In fact we have found that sage, for example, is equally as good dried as it is fresh and is even more

Fig. 8. Herb grower's work bench under gro-lights controlled by timer (right). Sage leaves are shown extreme left. Other herbs are, from left to right: chives, marjoram, rue, with geraniums behind, rosemary, and thyme (far right). A flat of lavender plants in expandable peat pots ready for repotting is seen in front of the timer. Also shown are: a bucket of vermiculite, a flat of potting soil (vermiculite, peat moss, sand, and loam), gardening tools, seed packages, pots and labels. Photo by Stephen T. Whitney.

GARDENING IN RESTRICTED AREAS—INDOORS AND OUT

Aloe
Bay, lemon verbena
Rosemary

---

powerful, so we do not bother to grow some herbs indoors if we have a sufficient stock dried in the pantry. But if you want a variety of fresh herbs for winter, select small plants for more successful results.

One herb every household should have growing indoors is a plant of *aloe.* This succulent plant thrives with neglect, dry conditions, and little light. It is said to have been one of Cleopatra's favorites. Aloe has been used in the treatment of radiation burns. For household emergencies — minor cuts and burns caused by hot grease — we find it indispensable. Break off a piece of the leaf and squeeze its glutinous juices on the sore. Its healing and soothing properties are remarkable, especially in a household of small children. Aloe will reproduce itself by developing miniature plants at the base of the parent. These can be separated and potted in a mixture largely of sand to increase your supply of home first-aid remedies.

Bay is another attractive and useful household herb. The plant is slow growing but can be kept for years potted in the house and sunk in the garden during the summertime. Increase the size of the pot every few years as the bay develops into a shrub. Its leaves are useful in cooking and can be dried for herb bouquets and wreaths.

Rosemary and lemon verbena con-front us with the greatest winter challenges. *Lemon verbena* is a relatively new arrival, having come to this country from South America by way of England in the late eighteenth century. Its distinctive lemon-scented leaves — fresh or dried — make it a useful household plant for cooking, teas, and sachets. Its care during the winter, however, may not be worth it. If the plant has spent a season out in the garden, be sure to pot it up a month before the first frost and leave it outside to get accustomed to its confinement for a week or ten days before bringing it into the house. Often the leaves of lemon verbena will dry and drop off when first brought inside. In this case, continue to water it sparingly and put it in a cool place until the dormant period is over and new growth has begun. Then allow it more light and water. If successfully cared for, this herb will develop into a sizable shrub, but the environment of most houses will tend to defeat its development.

Rosemary, however, is another story. While it must never be allowed either to dry out or to become too wet, this herb is one of the most rewarding to have in the house.

Topiary

A pot of rosemary lends itself to topiary work, and late winter is a good time to start it. First, select a plant with a woody, central stem.

Topiary
High-rise herbs
Wind and grime

Sink a metal rod into the pot as close to the stem as you can without disturbing the roots. Buy four or more wreath frames, 10 or 12 inches in diameter, from a local florist or make your own from metal coat hangers. Form these into a symmetrical orb and fasten the top and bottom where the circles meet either by binding with florist wire or soldering. Attach this to the points of contact with the vertical rod in the same way. Paint the whole armature black or dark green to prevent rust.

Bring the stems of the rosemary up the wire forms and attach them in several places with florist wire, taking care to leave enough room for the stems to develop without becoming pinched. As the plant continues to grow, train the main branches and thin out those that do not conform.

When the plant has largely covered the armature, this topiary will be an effective centerpiece. When summer comes, it can be sunk in the garden or left on the patio but be sure to continue watering it. If slightly pot-bound, rosemary will be encouraged to bloom.

High-Rise Herbs

If you live in a city apartment you can use your fire escape or roof terrace to keep your gardening activities alive during the summer.

As the amount of space available for growing plants is reduced, devotion to detail becomes more intensive. Distance from sources of soil, containers, and water supply may determine the extent of a high-rise garden. The higher one is, the greater the winds, the more reflected heat, and the less natural shade. More effort will be required to keep the moisture content high enough to combat these unnatural growing conditions.

Two other factors will affect the success of high-altitude gardens. One is the velocity of the winds. Plants with woody stems — sage, rosemary, tarragon — and others you trellis will do better than the more willowy kinds of herbs like dill, fennel, coriander, and anise. Another thing to consider is the amount of time you must devote to washing the foliage to combat urban grime which clog leaf pores and prevent growth.

These considerations may limit the selection of herbs you can raise successfully outside an apartment window, but at least you won't have predators to contend with.

Purple basil will make good accents; a rosemary topiary, a good focal point. Plant for either symmetry or a variation of heights and textures, but most of all plant for usefulness and personal satisfaction.

CHAPTER V

Harvesting and Drying

Preservation methods ... Harvesting ... Washing ...
Drying—in bunches, on racks ... Temperatures
... Seed and leaf herbs ... Oven and stove ... Bottling
and storage ... Freezing ... Annuals ... Perennials

HARVESTING AND DRYING
CHAPTER V

When we picture the low-beamed ceiling of the colonial keeping room — festooned with bunches of dried herbs, permeated with the aroma of half-remembered scents, and lit by the flickering hearth fire — we probably have a highly romanticized idea of what life was like when self-sufficiency dictated the economy. However attractive such a nostalgic picture is, reality tells us that the germicidal properties of hanging herbs may have been necessary in the days before modern sanitation. They look picturesque and release pleasant odors throughout the winter, but apart from some as decoration in the keeping room and kitchen, the bulk of our herbal harvest is neatly packed away and labeled for future use far from both dirt and sunlight. Most dried herbs will retain their essential oils for about a year only, even if carefully stored against the air; after that stock must be replaced, or cooking with herbs will result in a general sameness.

We dry herbs today by different techniques depending on the nature of the herb itself. There are three basic methods of drying to retain the color and volatile oils that characterize the species. One is to bunch the herbs loosely and hang them in an attic or shed; another is to spread out herbs on frames of screening or cheesecloth, stacked to allow air to circulate around them; and the third

uses application of some kind of supplemental heat to complete the drying process quickly before mold sets in.

Whichever method you use, the purpose is always the same: to dry herbs as soon as possible in order to retain their color and taste. Herbs can also be stored for later use by freezing them in small amounts, by layering them with salt in a crock or jar, or by infusing them in vinegar to retain the flavor but not the herb itself.

Harvesting

The best time to harvest most herbs is before they blossom. Cut them after the sun has dried the morning dew but before it gets so hot it dissipates the essential oils. Harvesting at this stage of growth will also force the plants to develop more leaves and allow a second or even a third cutting.

Most herbs should be washed after harvest to rid the leaves of garden dirt and insects. Rosemary and some of the crinkly-leafed herbs are particularly troublesome to wash as are low-growing herbs like parsley and thyme which catch the splash of ground water unless a heavy mulch is used. This is also the time to pick off any yellowed or spoiled leaves. Fill the sink with water and dunk the herbs, swishing them around gently so as not to bruise the leaves. When.

the rinse water is clear, place the harvest in a salad basket, colander, or sieve and let them drip dry in a shady spot outdoors for an hour or so. To avoid confusion harvest and wash only one kind of herb at a time.

The succulent stems of some large-leafed herbs like basil and lovage, or beebalm and catnip, can be strung on a clothesline in the shade where the breeze can reach them.

Drying

When all the excess water has evaporated, it is time to arrange the herbs for the actual drying process. Many large-leafed herbs can be loosely bunched, their stems tied with a string, and hung head down in a darkened and well-ventilated room like an attic or shed until it is time to store them. This will take from three days to several weeks, depending on the particular herb. A steady temperature of about 70 degrees is ideal. Direct sunlight will bleach the crop quickly, and since one of the benefits of home drying is to retain the color, be sure to cover the windows. Another way to block the sunlight is to cut out the bottom of a shopping bag and suspend the herbs within. This will also discourage dust from settling as the herbs dry.

We use an outbuilding to dry many of our herbs but make sure the door is closed at night, when dampness and lower temperatures threaten. A loft or attic is a better drying area, since it is less susceptible to nighttime cooling.

Bunch herbs like sage, basil, savory, marjoram, catnip, lovage, and the mints. For winter blossoms, do the same with the artemisias, yarrow, horehound, wild marjoram, and tansy.

The seed herbs — dill, fennel, coriander, anise, and caraway — should be harvested at the end of the summer. When the seeds begin to brown, they should be carefully watched to guard against the ravages of birds and wind. Clip the ripe seed heads into perforated paper bags, and hang them up to dry in a dark, well-ventilated place. When they are dry, either shake the bag to dislodge the seeds, pick them over by hand, or place your harvest on a clean sheet on the lawn and flail it. This will cause the seeds to drop and the chaff to be carried away by the wind. No matter how careful you are there will always be finicky handwork left — especially with anise — in order to separate the small stems from the equally tiny seeds before you use them. After flailing, spread the seeds on cheesecloth for four or five days more so they will be thoroughly dry before you bottle and store them. Again, remember to label each container accurately.

Some herbs can merely be left on screens to dry until you are ready to

Fig. 9. Fresh parsley drying over stove on screen racks. Parsley requires force-drying to prevent mold and to retain color and oils. The leaves are stripped from the stems, fluffed, dried, and then crumbled and stored. Photo by Stephen T. Whitney.

Drying
Oven and stove
Bottling and storage

process and store them. These include thyme, camomile, lavender, and tarragon. Thyme can be bunched if you prefer, but I consider it a waste of effort since it dries perfectly well stacked on screens. The woody stems will prevent matting and allow good air circulation.

Basil leaves too can be dried by first separating them from their stems and then laying them carefully on screens or cheesecloth. But basil always presents the problem of browning if the leaves are bruised, and we have had good success by hanging them in small bunches in the shed. If the bunches are too large, this herb may also mold. Whichever method, the drying process will take several weeks.

A few herbs will need some supplemental heat from the oven to dry them quickly and prevent mold. These are parsley, chives, chervil, and the weed of dill and fennel. Discard the larger stems from parsley, chervil, dill, and fennel, and spread the leaves or weed on a cookie tray or piece of screening cut to fit your oven. Chives should be cut into quarter-inch lengths with a sharp knife. Adjust the control to *warm,* insert the filled tray, and leave the oven door partially open. (If the aroma of the drying herb permeates the house, you are using too much heat and driving off the essential oils. Open the door further and fluff the herbs so the air will circulate.) Periodically rearrange the herbs on the screens to overcome their tendency to steam and mold before they start to dry.

If you have a wood-burning stove, you can set up a rack for screens, as we do, above and to either side of the stove. Each rack holds several layers of screens, and there is ample room for the air to circulate. As the drying proceeds we fluff the herbs and periodically lower each batch to the source of the heat.

When the leaves are brittle enough to crumble easily, they are dry. But don't store them until they have had a chance to cool and you have checked over the entire tray for dryness. Bottling a slightly damp herb will ruin your whole crop. On the other hand, moisture in the atmosphere can quickly be reabsorbed by the herb; so finish the process as soon as you can. If you find you have misjudged, and vapor is forming in the container, pull out the contents and start the drying procedure again.

When you have completed drying a batch of herbs — which can be a daily process for a large part of the summer if you have planted much variety — it is time to store the crop.

Bottling and Storage

We label and store dried herbs in a variety of containers — tins from

HARVESTING AND DRYING
Containers
Freezing
Other herb preserves

fruit cakes, large gallon glass jars with wide mouths and screw lids, canning jars, peanut butter jars (glass, not plastic, since the latter has an odor of its own). Nearly any container will do as long as it can be made airtight and kept in a dark, dry place. Paper bags should never be used for permanent storage because the essential oils will be lost in the paper, and you will be left with only a dried leaf.

It is best to keep your bulk harvest in the pantry or loft and only a representative sampling in small containers convenient to the stove.

Kitchen-herb containers can take many forms, as long as they are airtight (either with corks, screw-type lids, or ground-glass stoppers). They should also be opaque, unless they hold only very small amounts or are kept in a closed cupboard. Other containers can be squat antique boxes of wood or tinware, cutlery trays containing apothecary jars, an old-fashioned set of spice drawers, or even a special lazy susan or wicker basket that will make your array of herbs easy to reach and attractive. Or you can buy some imported canning jars of different colors, chemists' tubes stoppered with corks, pharmaceutical beakers for storing herb vinegars or little bags for *bouquets garnis.*

It is better to store whole leaves, stripped from their stems, than to crumble them or make mixtures ahead of time. In the first place, mixtures are essentially for the short-order cook. If they are convenient to the stove, their constant use will become just as monotonous as eating baked beans and hot dogs every Saturday night. The satisfaction of using home-grown culinary herbs lies in their variety, not their consistency. Another advantage to storing whole-leaf herbs is that the less you handle them, the more potent they remain.

Freezing

The herb fancier who has neither the room nor the produce to practice these drying techniques can freeze supplies of fresh herbs for winter use. Do this in small amounts and store them in labeled freezer bags or envelopes of waxed paper. When you are ready to use them, chop the herbs into your dish; they will be too limp when they thaw to use as garnish.

Other Herb Preserves

The Italians immerse fresh basil in pure cooking or olive oil, but this will only preserve the green leaves for several weeks. The colonials layered many kinds of fresh herbs with un-iodized salt in a wide mouthed jar or crock. This preserved them for a time but changed the color and would be a poor technique today for people on salt-free diets.

A Final Word

A final word about the harvesting and drying of herbs: In addition to the herbs you use daily for summer cooking, many annuals can be cut several times for drying during the season. Perennials can also be harvested two or three times but do not cut them late in the summer (in this climate we stop harvesting them generally by the first part of September) for they will need leaf growth to help get them through the winter. Otherwise, spring will come and you will not have any perennials left.

Labeling your dried harvest as you work may be picayune work but it is essential. Memory is tricky when it comes to identifying the aroma or taste of an herb you were familiar with when you saw it growing in the garden. Several mistakes in using dried herbs may cool your ardor and discourage rational experimenting. Wormwood does *not* taste the same as tarragon!

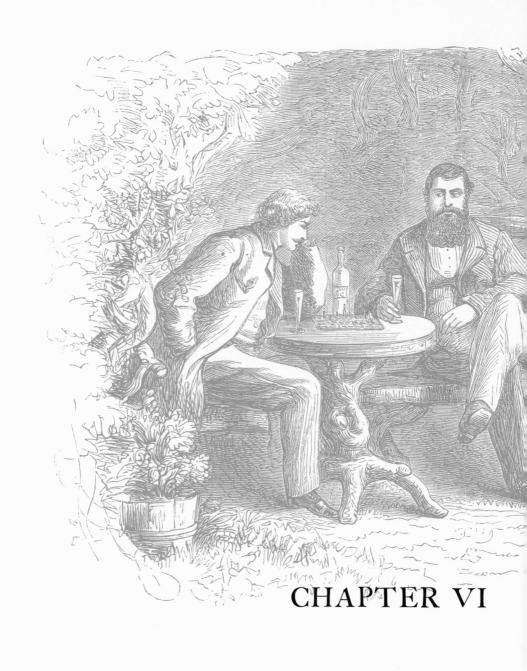

CHAPTER VI

Teas, Simples and Drinks

Herb teas or tisanes ... Bulk tea mixture ... Simples and specifics —
for colds; for stings, bruises and sprains ... Homemade eyewash,
ointment, and lotion ... Drinks, hot and cold ... May wine ... Liqueurs

TEAS, SIMPLES, AND DRINKS
CHAPTER VI

There are herbs growing just outside the door that can effectively ease the discomfort of lesser physical complaints neither serious nor persistent enough to warrant calling in the doctor. Though these remedies may not accomplish all that the ancient herbalists claimed, or effect cures as dramatically as today's patent medicines, we can use them safely and with good conscience. They cannot cause harm and may improve our health.

Herb Teas or Tisanes

Many who cannot drink coffee and China tea have turned instead to the mild, fragrant, and soothing herb teas. An aromatic tisane or infusion — a gentle brew generally golden in color, quiet in flavor — may be made from most herbs. The aromatic essences of the herbs are released by steeping the leaves in freshly boiled water for 5-10 minutes, depending on the herb and the flavor desired. If a tisane is too weak, it is better to use more herb than to steep it longer, for often the longer steeping will release a slightly acrid taste rather than a more concentrated one. Exceptions to this rule are found in the use of lemon balm, beebalm, and agrimony, which demand decocting, or boiling, in order to release the oils. If you use municipal water, be sure to let a supply stand overnight to allow the foreign flavors to dissipate before making tea.

Some of the most widely appealing sweet flavors are camomile, lemon balm, angelica (leaves), costmary, orange mint, peppermint, and spearmint. Rosemary and lavender teas, although unusual, should be tasted. Thyme and pennyroyal are old-fashioned stand-bys for that "out of sorts" feeling, and marjoram makes a lightly perfumed tisane. Sage was once enormously popular and deserves a wider following today, as does catnip. Dill is good taken at bedtime. Wild strawberry leaves produce a flavorful tea high in vitamin C.

Herb teas can be made in individual tea cups, but it is better to brew them in china, porcelain, or earthenware pots — never in metal, which alters the flavor. Use 3 tablespoons of fresh leaves or 1 tablespoon of dried for each cup of water. Add another tablespoon to the pot for good measure.

All herb teas (except mint teas) may be sweetened with honey, maple syrup, or sugar. A slice of lemon may be added, but never milk, since this will cloud the color and flatten the taste.

Dried herbs can also be used to transform China teas and give them an unusual appeal. Try making your own bulk tea mixtures by adding several kinds of herbs to the tea.

Fig. 10. Making a tisane. Green camomile. Yellow flower center is ready when white petals turn back. Separate heads from stalks (right and in jar) *and pour boiling water over the blossoms.* Photo by Stephen T. Whitney.

Here is one suggestion:

□ BULK TEA MIXTURE

Mix 1 quart dried leaves of angelica, lemon balm, costmary, orange mint, and camomile blossoms with the grated rinds of 1 lemon and 1 orange, 8 teaspoons China tea, 1 teaspoon ground clove, and dried calendula petals for coloring.

For more immediate use, simply add a leaf of dried rose geranium and 2 cloves to a pot of China tea. Green tea will be enhanced by dropping a sprig of spearmint and a few leaves of lemon verbena into the pot while the tea steeps. Or add grated orange and lemon peel, 3 tips of mint, and 1 of lemon balm for each cup of water. The combinations are endless, and like all experiments with herbs, you may find a particularly pleasing tisane just by chance.

On a wintry day, put a teaspoon of lemon juice, ¼ cup rum, and a bit of lemon peel into a glass or mug, and fill it with hot herb tea.

Simples

Many tea herbs can also be used for "simples," or home remedies, decoctions more concentrated than teas and in general more bitter tasting. Decoctions are made by boiling the seed or root of the herb for 3-5 minutes to release the resinous and

TEAS, SIMPLES AND DRINKS

Bitter tonic
Specifics
Cold remedies

---

bitter properties that help make the remedy effective. They were administered as doses — like the variety of spring tonics used to clear the blood, add pep and stamina, and stimulate the appetite after a long winter of limited diet. Bitter tonics made from dandelion roots, camomile flowers, mugwort, and wormwood were traditional in cases of loss of appetite; like gin and tonic, they stimulate the flow of gastric juices and saliva.

The principle of bitter tonic to stimulate the appetite has been used since the earliest times. You can make your own gin and bitters by putting ice in an Old Fashioned glass, adding a jigger of gin which has had wormwood blossoms infused in it, and twisting a strip of lemon peel over it, then dropping it in. This is also good for the digestion. Perhaps without being aware of it, the housewife was also infusing her family with the vitamins they sorely needed to combat the effects of too much meat and not enough fresh fruit and vegetables. Today simples can be used as styptics, antiseptics, stomach settlers, and mild sedatives, or soporifics.

Specifics

A "specific" is a treatment for a particular complaint, as opposed to a brew that might contain dozens of ingredients. Folklore is responsible for many of the following specifics which may or may not cure a symptom, but can provide some relief.

Dried costmary, angelica root, aniseed, and particularly mint are used as breath sweeteners.

Camomile, fennel seed, dill, and catnip teas are said to have a mild calmative effect.

The seeds of anise, fennel, cumin, coriander, angelica, and caraway will give a warm and pleasant sensation in the stomach and are good for children with colic.

Peppermint, boiled in milk, is used to settle the stomach and specifically to prevent seasickness.

Infusions of feverfew, hyssop, pennyroyal, peppermint, spearmint, summer savory, or yarrow can be used as mild stimulants.

For the onslaught of the common cold make a tisane of pennyroyal, hyssop, thyme, yarrow, lemon balm, or camomile — all of which will induce perspiration.

Colds must have especially plagued the early settlers, for there are many herbal recipes to relieve this ailment. A gargle to ease a sore throat can be made from sage.

☐ SAGE GARGLE
Make ½ pint of very strong sage tea, add honey, 1 tablespoon salt, vinegar, 1 teaspoon cayenne pepper.

Steep and strain before using.

Rosemary can be used for a similar gargle and can also be drunk as a tisane for a mild headache.

Comfrey root, sesame leaves, and coltsfoot, all demulcents, are combined with elecampane root and bloodroot for a simple to loosen the phlegm of the bronchial tubes and nasal passages.

The most everlastingly popular herb for treating coughs and colds is horehound. This can be used as a slightly bitter infusion, as a syrup, or boiled down into the form most generally known today, horehound candy.

□ HOREHOUND TEA

1 handful horehound leaves
1 teaspoon crushed anise seed
2 tablespoons honey (sugar or rock candy)
juice of 1 lemon
Put the leaves and seeds in an unchipped enamel or stainless steel kettle, add 1 quart boiling water, and simmer for 20 minutes. Remove from heat, strain, press leaves to extract all the liquid. Add sweetener, lemon juice. Cool and use.

□ HOREHOUND SYRUP

3 cups each of (dried) comfrey, horehound, tansy, and wormwood. Add 2 quarts water and let stand overnight or for several hours. Simmer until half boiled away. Strain and add 3 pounds granulated sugar and cook to a syrup.

□ HOREHOUND CANDY

Steep 1 ounce dried horehound (leaf, stem, and flower) for 2 minutes in 2½ quarts boiling water. Strain and squeeze through cheesecloth, allow to settle. Add 3 cups granulated sugar and 1 tablespoon cream of tartar to each 2 cups of liquid. Boil to 240°F. Add 1 tablespoon butter and continue boiling without stirring to 312°. Remove from heat and add 1 tablespoon lemon juice. Pour into buttered pan. When cool, mark into squares, roll in powdered sugar, and pack away in airtight jars.

Simples for relief of bee stings, bruises, and sprains were also common. Rubbing bee stings with the leaves of savory, hyssop, or lemon balm will ease the pain. A hot poultice of fresh parsley relieves other insect bites.

Camomile and comfrey poultices can be applied hot to external swellings. Stuff a small bag full of flowers or leaves, steep in boiling water, and apply. The medicinal properties of comfrey (formerly called boneset, bruisewort, or knitback) are presently underoing scientific investigation. This plant contains allantoin, which stimulates the formation of epithelial cells. A decoction of the

TEAS, SIMPLES AND DRINKS

Eyewash
Sunburn lotion
Ointment for cuts

---

root gives relief to stomach and duodenal ulcers. Beaten leaves are applied hot as a poultice to ease swellings, bruises, cuts, boils, and skin ulcers.

Steep hyssop leaves in hot water and press them to a bruise to remove the black and blue marks.

Oil of peppermint is still used to relieve toothaches because of its antiseptic and anesthetic properties. Garlic oil is also an antiseptic.

There are several herbs in our garden that are the basis of commercially important medicines. Digitalis, or foxglove, is still the primary plant drug used to regulate the action of the heart. Aconite, or monkshood, in minute amounts will depress an overly active heart. The roots of lily of the valley contain convallatoxin, the most potent of all the digitalis-like drugs, also present in toad skins. Both were historically prescribed to treat dropsy. This chemical is also used to treat glaucoma. *Only* doctors and pharmacists are knowledgeable enough to use these herbs *medicinally*. Their effects are very strong and thus dangerous. We grow them simply for their beauty.

Finally, some herbs can be used to manufacture homemade eyewashes, shampoo (see p. 102), and lotions for sunburn. Here are some simple rules.

☐ EYEWASH

For each application, pour ½ cup water that has been boiled for 5 minutes over ½ teaspoon each of camomile and fennel seed. Strain, cool, and use. Discard the remainder, if any, for it will not keep. Clary sage or eyebright can be substituted.

☐ SUNBURN LOTION

The tannin in rosemary, sage, and especially agrimony is the basis of this simple lotion. Infuse 3 heaping tablespoons of one of these herbs in ½ cup water for 30 minutes. In the top of a double boiler, heat ¼ cup sesame oil (which absorbs ultraviolet light better than other oils) and ¼ cup lanolin. Beat the herbal infusion into the oil slowly, making sure it is being accepted before adding more. When all of the infusion has been added, increase the beater speed and beat as you do egg whites, fluffing up the mixture, for 3-5 minutes.

☐ OINTMENT FOR CUTS AND SKIN IRRITATIONS

Decoct comfrey (chopped root) or calendula (flowers and leaves). Add this to an equal amount of olive or sesame oil. Simmer until all the water has evaporated. Add enough beeswax to solidify and melt again, stirring until well blended. (If a stronger ointment is desired, strain off the original herb and keep adding fresh material to the decoction until you have achieved the proper strength.) Remove the herb before allowing it to solidify for the last time.

Drinks

One of the many things the early settlers brought to this country was a distrust of drinking water, which was thought to be as unsafe here as in Europe. Rather than endanger their health in an unknown world, they continued to use stronger beverages, many of which contained herbs, until they were satisfied that the water was pure and harmless.

Here are some of the contributions we have found that herbs can make to modern drinks.

☐ LEMONADE
For each glass of iced lemonade, add a sprig of mint and a costmary leaf.

☐ MINT JULEP
Into a chilled julep glass put 4 leaves of fresh mint, 1 teaspoon each of sugar and water. Bruise the mint leaves and stir until the sugar has dissolved. Pack the glass with finely shaved ice, pour in a jigger of bourbon, and stir until the glass is frosted. Add another jigger of bourbon and garnish with a sprig of mint which has been dusted with powdered sugar.

☐ CLARET CUP
Into a glass put a sprig of borage and crush it with a wooden spoon or muddle. Add 1 tablespoon sugar, two orange slices and a slice of lemon. Half fill the glass with shaved ice, add claret to the rim and top with borage flowers.

☐ CIDER CUP
Crush a sprig of burnet or borage leaves in a glass. Grate a bit of nutmeg over it and add a slice of lemon, a sugar lump and ice. To this add ¼ cup sherry, 2 tablespoons brandy, lemon juice, 1 cup cider, club soda. Garnish with sprigs of borage.

☐ BLOODY MARY
Garnish this drink with a sprig of basil. When fresh basil is not available, add a pinch of powdered basil to each glass.

☐ PIMM'S CUP
Add burnet leaves with, or instead of, cucumber.

Coriander seed, hyssop, sweet marjoram, camomile, and wormwood blossoms are some of the herbs used in the manufacture of vermouth, from the German *vermut* or *wermuth* meaning wormwood. Wormwood was also used in the now illegal absinthe. However, you can make an interesting digestive without the harmful effects of absinthe as follows:

☐ FALSE ABSINTHE
Add a sprig of flowering wormwood stripped of leaves to a bottle of Pernod and let it steep. Put 3 ice cubes in a glass, half fill with the saturated mixture, add soda water and a twist of lemon peel.

What better way to greet the arrival of spring than by entertaining

TEAS, SIMPLES AND DRINKS

Punch recipes
May wine
Hot chocolate

a large group. Each of the following punch recipes will yield approximately 25 servings.

☐ MINT TULIP
Bruise a generous fistful each of fresh mint leaves and lemon balm (or ½ cup each chopped) in 1 cup water. Stir in 2 12-ounce cans of frozen concentrated lemonade and allow to stand for 1 hour. When ready to serve, strain the lemonade into a punch bowl, fill with ice, add 3 quarts of ginger ale, and garnish all with sprigs of mint.

☐ ORANGE MINT–CRANBERRY PUNCH
Simmer together for 10 minutes 1 cup fresh chopped orange mint, ½ cup sugar and 1 cup water. Add this to 1 quart cranberry juice, ½ cup lime juice. Chill. When ready to serve, pour over ice in a punch bowl, add 2 quarts ginger ale, and decorate with sprigs of fresh orange mint.

☐ TEA BASE HERB PUNCH
Pour boiling water to cover over a large handful each of lemon balm, mint, and borage. Let stand overnight. Strain and combine with sugar syrup (1 cup sugar boiled with ½ cup water for 5 minutes), 1 quart strong tea, 1 cup fruit juice (about 6 lemons and 3 oranges). Pour over a block of ice in a punch bowl and add 2 quarts ginger ale. Garnish with borage flowers or sprigs of mint.

Serving May wine is another traditional way of greeting the change of season. Although woodruff will not be in bloom here on May Day, as it is in Germany where this recipe originated, you can force blooms by bringing in potted plants in midwinter.

☐ MAY WINE
Into a jar put 6 bunches of fresh (1½ cups dried) woodruff and sprinkle them with 1 cup fine sugar. Let stand for 1 hour. Add ½ pint Cognac, 1 bottle Moselle wine, cover and let stand overnight in a cool place. When ready to serve, strain over a block of ice in a large punch bowl, add 3 more bottles of Moselle, 2 bottles of champagne or club soda. Float 1 cup whole fresh strawberries and sprinkle with tiny white woodruff blossoms.

Another stimulating and healthful punch is:

☐ LUNCHEON PUNCH
In a bowl combine 3 cups chilled tomato juice, 3 cups chilled clam juice, ¼ cup lemon juice, 2 tablespoons Worcestershire sauce, 2 dashes of Tabasco, ¼ teaspoon celery salt. Stir in 2 fifths of vodka and 12 ice cubes. Garnish with sprigs of fresh tarragon.

Finally, here are some hot drinks:

☐ MINTED HOT CHOCOLATE
Heat ½ teaspoon mint flakes in 4¾

cups milk until hot. Mix the following ingredients in a 2-quart pan and bring to a boil: ¼ cup sugar, ¼ cup cocoa, ¼ teaspoon,salt, ¾ cup water, 2 teaspoons vanilla extract. Boil and stir for 2 minutes. Pour heated milk through a sieve and strain out the mint leaves. Add milk to the syrup, stirring constantly. Serve hot with whipped cream topping. This serves 8.

☐ SLEEPER

For an individual drink, simmer 1 cup water for 5 minutes with 6 cloves, 6 coriander seeds, and 1 stick of cinnamon. Mix ½ cup rum, 1 tablespoon sugar, the juice of half a lemon in a mug and pour in boiling spiced water.

☐ NEGUS

A hot punch to serve eight. Mix 1 pint port (or any sweet wine) with 8 cubes of sugar, the juice of 1 lemon and 1 strip of rind, grated nutmeg, and 2 sprigs of costmary. Pour 1 quart boiling water over this in a pitcher or silver bowl and serve.

Liqueurs

Many common herbs are used in the manufacture of liqueurs and cordials. And most of the coriander grown commercially in this country is used, as well as angelica and juniper berries, for flavoring gin. Peppermint is used to make crème de menthe; caraway is in kümmel. Hyssop and angelica (along with some 98 other herbs and spices) contribute to the taste of chartreuse; anise is the basis of anisette. You can make your own liqueurs to serve over ice cream, desserts, or crushed ice. These will not be pure distillates, as fine brandies are, for syrup must be added.

☐ BASIC LIQUEUR

To make liqueurs in your kitchen, first steep the herb in brandy, then strain it out. To the herbed brandy, add sugar syrup. Make this by boiling 2 cups sugar in 1 cup water for 5 minutes. Filter your product and bottle.

☐ MINT BRANDY

Pick the herb early in the morning, wash it carefully in cool water taking care not to bruise the leaves. Put a handful into a 2½ quart jar and cover with 1 quart brandy. Let stand 48 hours and strain. Put ½ pound sugar in 2 cups water and bring to a boil. Pour this syrup into the jar, cover, and cool. Finally, strain and bottle.

For angelica liqueur, add 2 ounces chopped angelica stems to brandy and let it stand for 5 days. For anise-flavored liqueur, use tarragon infused in brandy for the same period of time. And you will undoubtedly try to invent many other teas, simples, and drinks; these are just a beginning, if you have a sense of adventure!

CHAPTER VII

Cooking with Herbs

Eggs ... Cheese ... Herb butters ... Sauces ... Dressings ... Marinades ...
Basting sauces ... Grilling with herbs ... Herb soups ...
Bouquets garnis ... Rice ... Breads ... Desserts ... Candy

COOKING WITH HERBS

CHAPTER VII

There is only one rule to observe in cooking with herbs: they must not mask the flavor of a dish, but rather enhance it. The recipes in this chapter are intended as a guide only — so that you can gain the confidence to experiment on your own. The use of herbs can become a creative adventure which — like your preference for color, music, or lifestyle — is a matter of personal judgment.

The chart on pp. 72 and 73 shows herbs others have found compatible with particular foods, but you will discover your own combinations with experience.

As a start, the common leaf herbs fall into two groups. The first group contains herbs whose flavors blend easily: parsley, chervil, chives, thyme, savory, basil, burnet, dill, fennel, and lovage. The second group includes dominant-flavor herbs such as tarragon, rosemary, marjoram, and sage. A herb mixture may contain several herbs from the first group, but only one from the second. Tarragon stands well alone but marjoram often needs the addition of thyme.

Herbs may be minced and added to cheese, butter and eggs or to vegetables, meats, poultry, and fish a few minutes before the end of cooking time; more can be sprinkled over the dish as a garnish. Cookbooks refer to these minced herbs as *fines herbes,* which in classic French cooking usually means a combination of tarragon, chives, chervil, and parsley. Herbs may also be added to stews, braised meat and vegetables, poached fish, and soup. Any dishes that cook over a relatively long period of time can be flavored with *bouquets garnis.* These herb bouquets are usually combinations of thyme, parsley, and bay leaf, tied with string if fresh or put into a cheesecloth bag if dried for easier removal before serving.

The volatile oils of herbs are released fairly quickly by heat, but if herbs are to flavor cold dishes — cheese, hors-d'oeuvres, butter, or drinks — the mixture should be allowed to stand a few hours or overnight in the refrigerator.

Your kitchen equipment should include a few basic tools such as kitchen scissors for mincing fresh herbs, a hand mill for grinding herb seeds and peppercorns, cheesecloth for making *bouquets garnis* and butcher's twine for tying them, and a mortar and pestle for powdering dried herbs and crushing seeds.

Most herbs can be used either fresh or dried. Until you establish how much flavoring you like, use 1 tablespoon of minced fresh herb for six servings, 1 teaspoon of dried leaf herb, or ½ teaspoon of powdered herb. Parsley is the exception; use it as generously as you like.

Begin by experimenting with eggs and cheeses. Individual herbs and combinations will affect a subtle transformation in their taste and character. But if the choice has not been a propitious one, the loss is not costly.

Egg Dishes

For eggs add one or more herbs (see chart) to the butter in the pan or to the egg before scrambling. Follow cooking with a generous sprinkling as garnish. Some of the combinations we like include the traditional *fines herbes* (tarragon, chives, chervil and parsley). Use about 1 teaspoon of fresh minced herbs or one-third teaspoon dried for each egg. The amounts given in the recipes that follow are for fresh herbs.

☐ **OMELETTES**
Here is a basic omelette recipe. To serve six people, prepare three small omelettes rather than one large omelette. For each omelette beat 3 eggs with 1 teaspoon cold water or milk and a pinch each of salt and pepper until blended. Add herbs. Melt 1 tablespoon butter in a pan or skillet on moderate heat. When foaming subsides, add mixture. With a fork pull the set portions toward the middle, lifting the edges so more of the liquid egg will cook. (Fill at this point if you are using one of the following variations.) Tilt the pan so the omelette slides, fold it over with a spatula, and turn it onto a heated serving dish.

● OMELETTE JARDINIERE
Chop chives, parsley, chervil, and a shallot to make 1 tablespoon. Add to egg mixture in bowl. Chop a few sorrel leaves and add to set eggs just before turning them.

● CHEESE OMELETTE
Fill set omelette with ¼ cup cottage cheese, 1 tablespoon chopped parsley and chives. *Or,* fill with ½ package (3 ounces) cream cheese, and 1 tablespoon chervil. *Or,* add 1 teaspoon caraway seed to ¼ cup finely diced or grated Muenster or Gruyère cheese and use as filling.

● SHAKER OMELETTE
Add 1 tablespoon parsley and chives to the egg mixture. Before turning, sprinkle 6 washed chive blossoms over the omelette.

● GREEN OMELETTE
Add ½ tablespoon minced fennel weed and 1 teaspoon chives to the egg mixture.

● BACON OMELETTE
Make a filling of 6 crumbled slices of bacon and 1 teaspoon chopped shallots.

● CRABMEAT OMELETTE
Add to the mixture 1 tablespoon finely chopped coriander leaves and parsley. Fill with 2 tablespoons crabmeat and a dash of lemon juice.

☐ **DEVILED EGGS**
Take 6 hardboiled eggs and split them lengthwise. Mix the yolks with

HERB CHART—WHAT TO USE WITH WHAT

EGGS	basil	dill	parsley	sorrel
	chervil	fennel	savory	tarragon
	chives	marjoram	shallot	thyme
CHEESE	basil	cumin seed	mints	savory
	caraway	dill	parsley	sesame seed
	chervil	lovage	poppy seed	shallot
	chives	marjoram	sage	tarragon
				thyme
SOUPS	basil	chives	marjoram	savory
	bay	cumin	mints	sorrel
	calendula	dill	parsley	tarragon
	caraway	fennel	rosemary	thyme
	chervil	lovage	sage	lemon thyme
FISH	basil	chives	marjoram	savory
	bay	dill	parsley	shallot
	chervil	fennel	rosemary	tarragon
				thyme
SHELLFISH	basil	dill	lovage	lemon thyme
	bay	garlic	parsley	thyme
	chervil	fennel	savory	tarragon
	coriander leaf		shallot	
VEGETABLES	anise	chives	lovage	sage
	basil	coriander	marjoram	savory
	bay	dill	mints	shallot
	caraway	fennel	parsley	tarragon
	chervil	garlic	rosemary	thyme
SALADS	basil	chives	marjoram	fresh sage
	borage	coriander leaf	mints	shallot
	burnet	dill	nasturtium	sorrel
	calendula	fennel	parsley	sweet cicely
	caraway	garlic	rosemary	tarragon
	chervil	lovage	savory	

HERB CHART—WHAT TO USE WITH WHAT

POULTRY	basil	chervil	garlic	sage
	bay	chives	marjoram	savory
	burnet	cumin	parsley	shallots
	caraway	dill	rosemary	tarragon
				thyme

BEEF	basil	cumin	marjoram	savory
&	bay	dill	parsley	shallot
VEAL	chervil	garlic	rosemary	tarragon
	coriander	lovage	sage	thyme

LAMB	basil	garlic	rosemary	tarragon
	bay	mint	parsley	thyme
	dill	marjoram	savory	

PORK	anise	caraway	fennel	sage
	basil	coriander	garlic	thyme
	bay	cumin	rosemary	

GARNISHES	burnet	chervil	fennel weed	parsley
	borage	chives	lemon balm	rosemary
	caraway leaf	dill weed	mints	sweet cicely

BREADS	anise	chives	marjoram	savory
	basil	cumin	parsley	shallot
	caraway	dill	poppy seed	tarragon
	coriander	fennel	rosemary	thyme
	chervil	garlic	sage	

FRUITS	angelica	dill seed	lemon balm	sweet cicely
	anise	fennel seed	mints	seed
	caraway seed		rosemary	

CAKES,	angelica	coriander seed	fennel seed	sesame seed
COOKIES,	anise	cumin	mints	
& PIES	caraway seed	dill seed	poppy seed	

DRINKS	anise	camomile	horehound	pennyroyal
& TEAS	beebalm	costmary	lemon balm	rosemary
	borage	dill	marjoram	sage
	burnet	fennel	mints	tarragon

COOKING WITH HERBS

Deviled eggs
Herb cheese
Cottage and cream

¼ cup mayonnaise, ¼ teaspoon salt and pepper, and add any of the following combinations (or others from the chart on pp. 72 and 73).

● 2 tablespoons minced cooked shrimp, 1 teaspoon tarragon, 1 teaspoon chives.

● ¼ cup minced cucumber, 1 teaspoon dill weed.

● ¼ pound chopped sorrel sautéed in 1 tablespoon butter for 10 minutes. Add this purée plus 1 tablespoon butter to the yolk mixture. Serve hot on toast.

● Use 1 cup cubed white meat of chicken, ½ tablespoon toasted almonds, 1 teaspoon tarragon and mayonnaise made with tarragon vinegar to stuff the egg whites. Sieve the yolks and sprinkle over the top of the stuffed eggs.

Herb Cheeses

Cottage cheese and cream cheese can both be flavored with herbs (see chart) and used as dips, celery stuffing, spreads, or fillings for tiny puff pastry hors-d'oeuvres or cocktail sandwiches. Thin dip mixtures with mayonnaise or cream and use with potato chips, tortillas, toast strips, and raw vegetables cut into bite sizes. Make the mixtures well ahead of time so the flavors will have time to develop.

□ HERB COTTAGE CHEESE

To ½ pound cottage cheese add any of the following combinations.

● 2 tablespoons minced chives, 1 tablespoon mayonnaise, salt, pepper.

● 1 tablespoon minced leaf herbs such as basil, dill, apple or orange mint.

● A pinch of powdered lovage, ¼ teaspoon crushed dill seed, ¼ teaspoon crushed caraway seed, 1 tablespoon minced parsley, 1 tablespoon grated onion, pinch of salt.

● 2 tablespoons minced fresh sage, 1 tablespoon sorrel or minced spinach, 1 teaspoon chives, salt.

● 1 teaspoon caraway seeds, ¼ cup soy bean sprouts.

● ½ tablespoon minced chives, ¼ teaspoon each of caraway, toasted sesame, and poppy seeds, 1 tablespoon mixed herbs (marjoram, basil, thyme, and sage).

● 1 teaspoon caraway, ½ teaspoon chives, ½ teaspoon minced garlic, salt, pepper.

□ HERB CREAM CHEESE

To 8 ounces of cream cheese add:

● 1 tablespoon parsley and 1 tablespoon dill weed.

● 1 tablespoon basil and 1 tablespoon fennel weed.

● 2 tablespoons *fines herbes.*

● Coat little balls of cream cheese by

rolling them in any of the mixtures, sesame seeds, or poppy seeds.

● 2 tablespoons minced pineapple, 1 tablespoon mint.

● ½ cup mayonnaise, 1 tablespoon horse-radish, 2 teaspoons chives.

● 12 chopped anchovy fillets, 2 tablespoons minced dill weed, 1 tablespoon chives.

● 1 cup sour cream, 1 cup crabmeat, 1 tablespoon nasturtium capers, 1 tablespoon chives, salt and pepper.

● ½ cup sour cream, 1 cup minced shrimp, 1 minced shallot, 1 tablespoon minced parsley, 1 tablespoon mixture of minced basil, thyme, and fennel seed.

● ¼ pound butter, ½ cup toasted sesame seed, 1 tablespoon poppy seed, 1 teaspoon mixture of minced summer savory, basil, and marjoram, ½ teaspoon salt and pepper.

Other cheeses can also be teamed with herbs to make good spreads.

□ HUNGARIAN CHEESEPOT

Mix a little butter with a feta-type goat cheese and roll into a ball. Dust the top with paprika and surround it with little mounds of capers, caraway seeds, and chopped onion or shallot to eat with the cheese on dark bread.

□ CHEESE SPREAD

Serve hot on toast strips or cold as a dip. Sauté 2 garlic cloves in 4 tablespoons oil. Add 2 cups tomato purée,

1 teaspoon dried basil, 2 tablespoons prepared herb mustard, 1 teaspoon sugar, ½ teaspoon marjoram, 2 sprigs minced rosemary, ½ pound grated sharp cheese, salt and pepper.

□ CHEDDAR-HERB MIXTURE

Grate 1 pound of sharp Cheddar cheese and mix with one of the combinations given below. Pack in pots, cover with melted butter, and refrigerate.

● ½ cup sherry, ¼ pound butter, 2 tablespoons minced chives, 3 tablespoons minced parsley, 1 tablespoon minced tarragon, salt and pepper.

● 3 ounces cream cheese, ¼ cup oil, 1 teaspoon powdered mustard.

● 1 teaspoon caraway seed, 2 tablespoons brandy, 2 tablespoons kirsch.

● 1 cup red wine, 2 teaspoons crumbled dried sage or 2 tablespoons minced fresh sage.

Herb Butters

Keep herb-flavored butters handy in the refrigerator. Their uses are limitless. Fry breakfast eggs in herb butter, add it to scrambled eggs when almost set, or top an egg to be baked with a tablespoon pat of herb butter. Use in sandwiches, in French bread, on hot biscuits; add to cooked vegetables or spread on hot cooked meats and fish.

□ BASIC HERB BUTTER

Mix ¼ cup butter with 1 tablespoon

COOKING WITH HERBS

Herb butters
Herbed vegetables

---

fresh herb or 1 teaspoon dried and a squeeze of lemon. (If you use dried herbs, mince fresh parsley or spinach leaf for color and mix in well.)

Since so many herbs are compatible with cooked vegetables, here are some suggested combinations to guide you. *Fines herbes* are at home with nearly any vegetable. Cook such vegetables as carrots, salsify, beets, beans, peas, and boiled cabbage until barely tender in lightly salted water. Stir in the herb butter 5 minutes before serving.

□ ZUCCHINI WITH *FINES HERBES*
Trim the ends of 6 small whole zucchini and place in a baking dish with 3 tablespoons *fines herbes* butter, 2 tablespoons lemon juice, salt, and pepper. Cover closely and bake 30 minutes in a 325° oven. Serves 6.

Basil, commonly used with tomatoes, is good with other vegetables, too. Try it with summer squash, Italian beans, onions, peas, eggplant, and:

□ HERBED GREEN BEANS
In a saucepan sauté ½ cup each of chopped onion and celery and 1 clove crushed garlic in 3 tablespoons butter until tender but not colored. Stir in young whole green beans, cover, and cook 10-15 minutes very slowly. Stir in 2 or 3 tablespoons basil butter.

Dill and sour cream are a famous partnership, But try it also with beets, boiled potatoes, or cucumbers.

□ DILLED CUCUMBER STICKS
Boil cucumber sticks in salted water for 5 minutes and dress with dill butter.

□ DILLED SUMMER SQUASH
Parboil for 5 minutes 6 medium squash. Drain, and chop coarsely. Sauté this with 2 tablespoons minced onion in 3 tablespoons dill butter until soft. Mix with ½ cup sour cream, more minced dill, salt and pepper. Put in buttered dish, sprinkle with bread crumbs, and bake 15 minutes in a 350° oven.

Marjoram-Thyme-Parsley is a good combination for many vegetables, particularly beans, brussel sprouts, lima beans, spinach, and leeks, not to mention mushrooms.

□ STUFFED MUSHROOMS
Wash and dry 1 pound large mushrooms and cut off the stems. Chop stems and sauté them in 1 tablespoon butter with 1 tablespoon chopped shallot for 5 minutes. Add 2 tablespoons marjoram-thyme-parsley butter, ½ cup dry bread crumbs, 1 beaten egg, and salt and pepper to taste. Sauté the caps in butter until golden. Put on a baking sheet, fill with the stuffing, sprinkle with lemon juice and dot with marjoram butter. Bake for 5 minutes in a 450° oven.

Mint. Boil new potatoes with a sprig of fresh mint. Add mint butter and chives to mashed potatoes, peas, and yellow summer squash sautéed with a clove of garlic.

☐ CARROTS IN MINT BUTTER

Cut carrots into matchstick lengths and cook in salted water until barely tender. Drain and sauté slowly in 2 tablespoons plain butter and 1 teaspoon sugar. Add 2 tablespoons mint butter 5 minutes before serving.

Savory is cooked with string beans, especially by German cooks. Savory butter is also used on carrots, cabbage, lentils, and potatoes.

☐ SAVORY TOMATOES

Halve 6 tomatoes. Remove and save the pulp. Turn the shells upside-down to drain. Cut crusts from 3 slices of white bread. In a bowl combine cubed bread, ¼ cup brown sugar, salt, pepper, the tomato pulp, and one-third cup melted savory butter. Fill the shells with this mixture, place on a shallow pan, and bake about 20 minutes at 350°.

Use *rosemary* with braised leeks and onions, pan-fried potatoes, turnips and rutabagas, and in vegetable casseroles.

☐ SPINACH WITH ROSEMARY

In a saucepan cook 2 chopped scallions in ¼ cup rosemary butter for several minutes. Add to the pan 3 pounds washed chopped spinach, cover and cook about 5 minutes. Season with salt and pepper to taste and sprinkle generously with minced parsley.

Sage or Sage-Thyme is good with baked stuffed potatoes, hashed brown potatoes, rutabagas, braised onions, or scalloped tomatoes. And also with:

☐ BAKED WINTER SQUASH

Halve and seed acorn or other winter squash and place cut-side down in a pan of water. Bake at 400° for 30 minutes. Turn squash over, place 1 tablespoon sage or sage-thyme herb butter in each cavity, sprinkle with bread crumbs, and bake until tender.

Tarragon and parsley add an interesting accent to braised fennel bulb, beets (add a touch of sugar and a dash of vinegar), carrots, cauliflower, salsify, asparagus, broccoli, or peas.

☐ PEAS IN TARRAGON BUTTER

Place 2 pounds fresh peas (or 1 package frozen peas) in a pan with some lettuce leaves, 1 teaspoon each of salt and sugar, a dash of pepper, 6 tablespoons tarragon butter, 1 tablespoon minced shallot or onion, and 2 tablespoons chicken bouillon or water. Cover and cook gently for 20 minutes or until tender. Allow less time for frozen peas.

Herb butters can also be added to spaghetti.

COOKING WITH HERBS

Herbed spaghetti
Herb-seed butter
Poultry and meats

☐ HERBED SPAGHETTI

Mince enough thyme or savory, chives, parsley, basil, and marjoram to make ¼ cup. Mix this with ¼-cup butter and melt it in ¼ cup olive oil with several cloves of crushed garlic. Pour over hot spaghetti and toss with Parmesan cheese.

☐ HERB-SEED BUTTERS

Butters made with herb seeds flavor vegetables in a variety of ways. Toss boiled, drained egg noodles with ½ cup melted butter to which you have added 1 tablespoon caraway seed or poppy seed and ½ cup slivered, toasted almonds, or, just add ½ cup toasted sesame seeds to the butter. When serving baked potatoes, crush 12 coriander seeds, cream with butter, and form the mixture into walnut-sized balls. You might also serve butter balls made with dill, chives, and parsley and let the diner take his choice.

Before serving meat, poultry, or fish that is broiled, sautéed, or grilled, top with herb butter (see chart, pp. 72 and 73) and let sit for a minute in a warm oven. Use 1 tablespoon herb butter for each chop, patty, or piece of chicken and more for a steak.

Rather than use bread-crumb stuffings, stuff thick chops and whole baked or broiled fish with herb butter, or insert softened herb butter between the skin and breast meat of poultry. Do this by putting herb sprigs in the cavity, loosen the breast skin with a pointed knife, and insert a thin layer of butter between the skin and meat. During roasting this acts as an automatic baster, and in broiling the tender herbs are not burned in the process of flavoring the meat.

☐ CHICKEN KIEV

After removing the skin, halve and bone 3 chicken breasts. Flatten each piece by pounding between waxed paper. Wrap the meat around a finger-sized piece of herb butter. (Try chive, *fines herbes,* or burnet-thyme butters for this recipe.) Coat with flour, dip in beaten egg, and roll in bread crumbs. Refrigerate for a few hours. Before serving fry in deep fat until golden.

When you have sautéed or roasted meat or poultry, remove it to a heated platter and make a sauce with herb butter. This can be done with steaks, chops, liver, chicken pieces, hamburgers, and roasted beef and chicken. Tarragon is particularly good with chicken and beef, rosemary with lamb, marjoram and thyme with veal and liver. But use the chart and experiment.

☐ HAMBURGER WITH DEGLAZED HERB SAUCE

Sauté 2 pounds hamburger patties. Remove them to a serving dish and pour the fat from the skillet. Add ½ cup beef stock or dry red wine, and boil down rapidly scraping all the bits of meat and juices into the liquid. When reduced to almost a syrup, take from the heat and add 2 or 3 tablespoons *fines herbes* butter. Pour this sauce over patties and serve.

Because some shellfish and fish fillets take such a short time to cook, they can be baked in herb butters. Place clams or oysters on the half-shell on a cookie sheet, dot with herb butter and bread crumbs and broil about 4 minutes or until the edges curl. Use thyme-tarragon-parsley-minced garlic butter for clams; parsley-chive-chervil for oysters. Place shrimps or scallops in a baking dish, cover with a generous amount of melted herb butter, sprinkle with Parmesan cheese, and bake for 15 minutes. Chervil and chives are good with scallops; basil-tarragon-parsley with shrimp.

☐ FISH FILLETS BAKED IN HERB BUTTER

Pour ½ cup melted marjoram-thyme-parsley butter over 2 pounds fish fillets in a baking pan. Add ½ cup sliced stuffed olives and bake in a 350° oven until the sauce bubbles and the fish flakes.

Piping hot biscuits are delicious with herb butters. Corn bread takes on a different character when served with sage-thyme butter. Cut it into finger-sized pieces, dip in melted herb butter, place on a baking sheet, and bake for about 5 minutes in a 450° oven.

☐ FRENCH BREAD

Slice the bread nearly through and butter before wrapping in foil and baking in a 350° oven for 20 minutes. One butter combines ½ cup butter with 1 teaspoon rosemary, 1 teaspoon chives, 1 teaspoon thyme, 1 teaspoon marjoram, and salt.

☐ RYE BREAD

Use a butter of 1 tablespoon tarragon, 1 teaspoon thyme, 2 tablespoons parsley, a pinch each of rosemary and sage, and 1 tablespoon minced shallot or onion.

Sauces

Herbs added to any of the half-dozen families of sauces conjure up difficult French names and impossibly long preparations, but with a blender and a few common ingredients, you can create a sauce to make a simply prepared food into a classic dish.

Mayonnaise and Hollandaise go well with most cold meats, vegetables, and salads. They are particularly good on hot or cold fish, stuffed (deviled) eggs, and hot vegetables like broccoli, asparagus, cauliflower, and milkweed blossoms.

COOKING WITH HERBS

Mayonnaise
Variations
Hollandaise

□ **BASIC BLENDER MAYONNAISE**
In a blender combine 1 egg, ½ teaspoon salt, 1 teaspoon dry mustard, a dash of pepper, 1 teaspoon lemon juice or vinegar, and ¼ cup oil. Cover and turn on high. Slowly pour in three-quarters cup oil and blend until thick. Add 1 teaspoon more lemon juice or vinegar. This makes 1¼ cups mayonnaise.

● GREEN HERB MAYONNAISE
Add 1 tablespoon minced parsley, ½ tablespoon each of chives, tarragon, dill and chervil. Use with vegetables.

● TARTAR SAUCE
Add 1 tablespoon each of chopped dill pickle, shallot, minced parsley, tarragon, and chervil, 1 teaspoon mustard, and 1 teaspoon lemon juice. Use with fish.

● REMOULADE SAUCE
Add 1 tablespoon each of chopped parsley and chervil, 1 teaspoon minced tarragon, ½ teaspoon anchovy paste, 1 tablespoon finely chopped pickles, 1 teaspoon prepared mustard, and some capers. This goes well with shellfish, celery-root salad, and cold veal.

● SOUR CREAM SAUCE
Add ½ cup sour cream, 2 tablespoons minced chives, parsley, and dill weed, salt and pepper to taste. Use with fish, eggs, cucumber, or tomato salad.

● COLE SLAW SAUCE
Add ½ cup sour cream, 1 teaspoon crushed fennel seeds, ¼ to ½ cup sugar, lemon juice or vinegar.

The next three sauces are good as dips or to pour over the halves of stuffed eggs to serve as a first course or lunch.

● CURRY MAYONNAISE
Add 2 tablespoons curry powder, 1 tablespoon each of minced parsley, chives, and green onions.

● TOMATO SAUCE
Add ¼ cup tomato purée, ½ teaspoon lemon juice, ½ teaspoon minced lemon thyme, and 1 teaspoon minced basil.

● HERB MAYONNAISE
Add ½ cup mixture of chopped parsley, tarragon, and chervil combined with ½ clove of crushed garlic and ½ cup sour cream.

□ **BASIC BLENDER HOLLANDAISE**
In a blender put 3 egg yolks, 2 teaspoons lemon juice, ¼ teaspoon salt, and a dash of pepper. Heat ½ cup butter until it begins to foam. Turn blender to high and very slowly pour in the butter. Add herbs. If not to be served immediately, place sauce in a heavy bowl in a pan of barely warm water.

● TARRAGON HOLLANDAISE
Add 1 tablespoon tarragon or tarragon-parsley-chives. Serve with asparagus, cauliflower, broccoli, or artichokes, with seafood or eggs.

Fig. 11. Kitchen herbs ready to use. Orange mint, curly mint, and lovage hanging from pegs (l. to r.). The box holds white and golden feverfew.

COOKING WITH HERBS

Bearnaise
Pesto
White sauce

● BEARNAISE SAUCE

In a saucepan combine 2 tablespoons white wine with 1 tablespoon tarragon vinegar, 2 teaspoons minced shallots and fresh tarragon. Simmer until only about one tablespoon of liquid is left. Add to Hollandaise. Good on broiled steaks, chicken, eggs, and fish.

● CHORON SAUCE

Add 3 tablespoons tomato paste to Béarnaise. For broiled meats and fish.

Although technically not one of these sauces, pesto is a must for anyone who loves the taste of basil. Serve it over spaghetti that has been tossed with oil and butter; fill tomatoes with it; use it as a dip for cold vegetables or as a sauce on hot beans, squash, eggplant, broccoli, and cauliflower. Float a tablespoonful per cup on vegetable soups.

□ PESTO

Put into a blender 2 or more cloves of garlic, 1½ cups fresh basil leaves (if you use dried, add parsley or spinach for color), ¾ cup Parmesan cheese, ¼ cup pine nuts or walnuts, and three-quarters cup olive oil. Blend until perfectly smooth.

White Sauce Family

White sauces make economical meals of left-over poultry, fish, and eggs. Pour them over poached fish or chicken, sprinkle with cheese, and brown a few minutes under the broiler for an elegant dish. Béchamel is made with milk, velouté with broth (beef, chicken, or fish stock), with the option of adding cream.

□ BASIC WHITE SAUCE

Melt 2 tablespoons butter in a heavy-bottomed pan. Sauté a shallot or small minced onion in this; add 2 tablespoons flour and stir until the mixture foams without browning (about 2 minutes). Add 1 cup boiling liquid (milk or broth) and stir while bringing the mixture to a boil. Boil for 1 minute and season. Add a few tablespoons of heavy cream and lemon juice to velouté, if desired. The sauce is now ready for herbs and additional flavoring.

● TARRAGON SAUCE

Simmer ½ cup dry white wine, 2 tablespoons tarragon, 1 tablespoon minced green onion or shallots for 10 minutes. Strain into béchamel and simmer 2 minutes. Stir in additional tarragon just before serving. If you want to substitute 2 tablespoons *fines herbes* for the tarragon, you will have sauce Chivry.

● CURRY SAUCE

Add 2 tablespoons curry powder.

● SAUCE AURORE

Add 2 tablespoons tomato paste and 2 tablespoons basil.

● DILL SAUCE

Add 2 tablespoons or more dill weed

to velouté made with chicken stock for poultry or with fish stock (or with half milk, half clam juice, or half white wine, half clam juice) for fish.

● CORIANDER SAUCE

Use cream in the béchamel and add to it ½ cup sour cream, 1 tablespoon dill weed, 1 teaspoon each of basil, tarragon, coriander leaf, salt and pepper to taste. Use this with poultry. (Some people find the taste of coriander leaf offensive, but in Mexico, where coriander is called *cilantro,* it is used much like parsley, and in Eastern and Chinese cooking where it is called *yuen-sai,* both the seed and the leaf are used.)

Brown sauces serve much the same purpose as white sauces but are used mainly for meats and sometimes poultry.

□ BASIC BROWN SAUCE

Melt 1½ tablespoons butter in a saucepan and add 1½ tablespoons flour. Stir over low heat until very smooth and tan colored. Add 2 cups good beef consommé. Bring to a boil and cook 5 minutes, stirring. Lower the heat and simmer gently for 30 minutes. Season with salt and pepper to taste.

● SAUCE BORDELAISE

In a saucepan simmer 2 minced shallots or a small onion in ½ cup red wine until reduced to about 2 table-spoons. Add brown sauce and simmer 10 minutes. Add 1 tablespoon minced tarragon. This is the classic sauce for steaks.

● PIQUANT SAUCE

Simmer 3 tablespoons dry white wine, 1½ tablespoons vinegar, and 1 minced shallot until reduced to 2 tablespoons. Add to brown sauce, bring to a boil, and simmer for 5 minutes. Add 1½ tablespoons minced sour pickle, 1 tablespoon each of minced chives, and parsley, and 1 teaspoon tarragon. Serve with roast pork, chops, or left-over sliced meats.

Oil and vinegar dressings are usually made in the relationship of 3 parts oil to 1 part vinegar in easily usable amounts.

□ BASIC OIL AND VINEGAR DRESSING

Mix three-quarters cup oil, ¼ cup vinegar, ½ teaspoon salt, a fresh grating of pepper, ¼ teaspoon dry mustard, and 2 or 3 tablespoons minced herbs. Add the herbs 5-10 minutes before using.

● SAUCE AFRICAINE

Substitute the juice and grated rind of 2 lemons for the vinegar in the basic recipe, and add a dash of Tabasco, 2 minced garlic cloves, ½ teaspoon each of coriander, ground cumin, dry mustard, paprika, and 1 teaspoon sugar. Dress a green salad with this and pieces of crumbled bacon.

COOKING WITH HERBS

Herbed dressings
Salads
Marinades

● FRUIT SALAD DRESSING
Substitute 2 tablespoons lemon juice for the vinegar in the basic recipe, and add 1 teaspoon sugar and minced rosemary or tarragon. Use with salads of orange, grapefruit, or avocado sections.

● DILL-SOUR CREAM DRESSING
Add 1 cup sour cream, 1 clove crushed garlic, 1 teaspoon sugar, 1 tablespoon minced burnet, and 2 tablespoons minced dill weed. Use this to dress cucumber, a tomato salad, cooked broccoli, fish, or eggs.

● MINT DRESSING
Use mint vinegar, or bruise 2 dozen mint leaves with your fingers and soak them in vinegar for 30 minutes before making the dressing. For cold sliced lamb, peas, carrots, cauliflower, and fruit salads.

● HERBED MUSTARD DRESSING
Add 1 tablespoon prepared mustard and 2 tablespoons *fines herbes.* For cold sliced meats or salads.

☐ VEGETABLES VINAIGRETTE
Choose asparagus, artichoke, leeks, celery, fennel, broccoli, raw mushroom caps, cucumbers, cauliflower buds, cooked dried beans (lentil, kidney, and chick peas), green beans, or small zucchini cut diagonally. Simmer the vegetable in salted water or stock until only just tender. Cool and pour dressing over it, allowing it to marinate for at least 30 minutes.

Good for winter salads and summer vegetable treatment.

Salads

In making green salads, mince herbs right into the lettuces. We often add them in such quantities that the result is a true herb salad. The first green salad makings to appear in the spring are sorrel, cress, mint, chervil, sweet cicely leaves, and burnet. A typical summer salad would include at least ¼ cup minced parsley, burnet, borage cut in paper-thin strips, chives, basil, dill, a touch of savory, minced nasturtium leaves, nasturtium buds, calendula petals, and perhaps a touch of minced mint or fresh sage. Tarragon is such a perfect salad herb that we use it solely with chives, chervil, fennel, or dill weed, if not alone with chives. All this is tossed with dressing and lettuces in a large garlic-rubbed wooden trencher just before it is to be eaten.

Marinades and Basting Sauces

Minced and added to casseroles, meat loaf, or to basting sauces and marinades, herbs flavor foods as they cook. Those dishes which cook in liquid (soups, stews, fricassees, braised meats and vegetables, fish, and shellfish) are conveniently flavored with a herb bouquet.

If you sprinkle fresh, tender herbs over a slow-cooking roast or meat that requires a very hot broiler, one result will obviously be some very charred herbs. Basting the meat as it cooks with a herb sauce prevents this.

□ BASIC BASTING SAUCE

Simmer together for 10 minutes 1 cup beef stock (chicken stock with chicken), ½ cup dry wine, 2 tablespoons fresh herbs, and 1 clove of minced garlic (optional).

● LAMB

Use red wine and 1 tablespoon rosemary; 2 tablespoons mint; *or,* a sprig of rosemary, 2 teaspoons mint, and 1 tablespoon basil.

● BEEF

Use beef broth, red wine, 1 tablespoon thyme; *or* 1 tablespoon savory and 1 crumbled bay leaf.

● PORK

Use white wine, garlic, 1 tablespoon rosemary, ½ teaspoon aniseed, a dash of nutmeg; *or,* use tomato juice instead of broth, a scant teaspoon cumin seed and 3 tablespoons parsley.

● POULTRY

Use white wine or vermouth, 1 tablespoon each of parsley and tarragon.

Any meat to be baked or broiled will benefit by being left for a time, usually overnight, in a marinade which adds flavor and tenderizes at the same time. Then pour the marinade over the oven roast or use as all or part of the liquid in braising meats.

□ BASIC MARINADE

Mix 1 cup oil, ½ cup wine, vinegar, or lemon juice; salt to taste, 10 crushed peppercorns, 1 clove of garlic, and herbs.

● BEEF

Use red wine, 1 bay leaf, 1½ teaspoons basil and oregano (wild marjoram); *or,* 1½ teaspoons rosemary or marjoram, 1 bay leaf, and red wine.

● LAMB

Use red wine with 1 tablespoon each of mint, parsley, and a sprig of rosemary; *or,* red wine with 1 bay leaf, 1 chopped onion, 1 tablespoon parsley, 1 teaspoon each of crushed coriander and cumin seed.

● PORK

Use white wine with 1 teaspoon thyme, ½ teaspoon caraway seed: *or,* white wine with 1 teaspoon each of thyme, parsley, and basil.

● POULTRY

Use white wine or vermouth and 1 tablespoon of either basil, tarragon, or rosemary.

● FISH

Use white wine, ½ bay leaf, and 1 tablespoon dill or fennel weed; *or,* 1 tablespoon tarragon or thyme.

Grilling with Herbs

Marinating is most appreciated when grilling steaks, chops, and

COOKING WITH HERBS

Meats and fish
Vegetables
Dessert

kabobs. You can be inventive, though, and prepare a whole meal on the grill with herbs and thereby use the fire efficiently. Here are some ideas.

☐ **FISH**
Marinate chunks of white fish for 10 minutes in sherry. Alternate these on a skewer with bay leaves and chunks of cucumber and grill.

☐ **STEAKS AND CHOPS**
Rub dried herbs (rosemary, tarragon, thyme, or crumbled bay leaves) into the meat and allow to sit at least 2 hours before grilling. Sear the meat on both sides and arrange on branches of fresh herbs to finish cooking. To flavor gently with herbal smoke, throw herb branches onto the fire during the last few minutes of cooking. Try the following: rosemary for beef; fennel for fish; thyme, fennel, and bay leaves for pork; and tarragon for chicken.

☐ **VEGETABLES**
Wrap vegetables in heavy foil and roast in the coals.

● **EGGPLANT**
Split lengthwise, sprinkle with oil, salt and pepper, 1 clove of minced garlic, a slice of onion, and 1 teaspoon of minced thyme or mint.

● **MUSHROOMS**
Salt and pepper 6 caps and add 1 tablespoon tarragon butter.

● **TOMATO**
Halve, salt and pepper, sprinkle with oil and 1 teaspoon chopped parsley and basil.

● **ZUCCHINI**
For each small, whole zucchini, salt and pepper, and sprinkle with oil and 1 tablespoon mixed marjoram, thyme, and parsley.

In *King Henry V,* Shakespeare talks about eating roasted apples with a dish of caraway seeds, which was a popular Elizabethan custom. It provides a delightful way to use those still glowing coals.

☐ **DESSERT GRILL**
Dip thick slices of cored apple into melted butter and arrange on a hinged broiler or on the grill. Cook for a few minutes and turn. Sprinkle with sugar and serve with small dishes of caraway seeds.

Soups

Everything benefits from the addition of herbs, but soups, especially canned soup, *require* them! Crush dried herbs into the soup a few minutes before serving, or mince fresh herbs into the soup as a flavorful garnish. Try thyme, savory, or mint in green pea soup; dill weed or seed in tomato; lemon thyme, thyme, or sage in fish chowder; chervil or rosemary in chicken; basil or costmary in vegetable; chives in cream-of-asparagus as well as vichyssoise; calendula petals in chicken or vegetable soups; savory in lentil or black bean.

What really transforms a can of soup into gourmet fare is the addition of a dash of herb brandy. Put a few sprigs of the herb (tarragon, rosemary, sage, or thyme) into a small bottle and cover with brandy. Put it closely stoppered into a dark place and shake it every day for a week or two.

Of course, there is nothing like homemade herbed soups. Here are some you should try.

☐ HERB SOUP

Melt 2 tablespoons butter in a saucepan, add ¼ cup minced green onion, 2 tablespoons each of minced chives, chervil, sorrel, parsley, ½ tablespoon tarragon, 1 cup shredded celery, and cook for 5 minutes. Add 1 quart broth, salt and pepper to taste, and cook 15 minutes. Add one-third cup dry white wine. Put a piece of toast in each bowl, sprinkle with Parmesan cheese, and ladle the soup over it.

☐ ROSEMARY AND SORREL SOUP

Sauté 1 chopped onion in 4 tablespoons butter, add 3 cups chopped sorrel leaves, 2 sprigs of rosemary, 1 quart chicken broth, and simmer for 15 minutes. Add 3 cooked mashed potatoes and simmer an additional 15 minutes. Add 1 cup cream, bring to a simmer, and sprinkle with minced parsley before serving.

☐ CUCUMBER-CHERVIL SOUP

Sauté 2 chopped scallions in 4 tablespoons melted butter in a saucepan until soft but not brown. Add 3½ cucumbers (peeled, seeded, and sliced), 1 cup water, salt and pepper. Simmer 15 minutes. Stir in 3 tablespoons flour mixed to a paste with a little cold water, and 3 cups chicken broth. Stir until it comes to a boil and simmer for 5 minutes. Blend it or put it through a sieve, return to saucepan, and add ½ cup minced chervil and 1 cup cream. Serve hot or cold.

☐ GAZPACHO

Put into a blender or chop in a bowl 6 tomatoes (peeled and seeded), 1 clove of garlic, 1 large onion, 2 small cucumbers, 1 green pepper, ¼ cup olive oil, 2 tablespoons red wine or (vinegar or lemon juice), salt and pepper, and ½ teaspoon powdered cumin seed. Blend or mix briefly and chill. Serve with little bowls of croutons, chopped hard-boiled eggs, parsley, basil, chopped pepper, tomato, and celery for the guests to use as garnish.

Bouquets Garnis

Herb bouquets also flavor soups and chowders as well as poached chicken and fish, chicken fricassee, braised meats, stews, and boiled beef. Tie sprigs of fresh herbs with

COOKING WITH HERBS

Herb bouquets
For poultry
For beef

---

butcher's twine or place dried herbs in a 4-inch square of cheesecloth and tie. Leave a loop in the string to make removal of the bouquet easier before serving. Each bouquet will flavor up to 2 quarts. The basic recipe will make two small bags or *bouquets garnis.*

□ BASIC HERB BOUQUET

Fresh: 2 sprigs of thyme, 4 to 6 sprigs of parsley, and 1 bay leaf. Dried: 1 broken bay leaf, 2 teaspoons thyme, and 2 tablespoons parsley.

The variations that follow use *dried* herbs.

● TOMATO

For soup or sauce: 1 bay leaf (broken in 2 pieces), 2 cloves, 1 teaspoon lemon thyme, 1 teaspoon basil, 1 tablespoon parsley, and ½ teaspoon crushed lovage.

● ● TOMATO SOUP

Simmer for 30 minutes 3 cups tomato juice, a slice of onion, and 1 soup bag (above). Remove bag and onion, add 2 cups beef broth, a pinch of sugar, and salt and pepper to taste. Heat and serve with whipped cream that has been lightly salted and flavored with minced chives. (Substitute cream for broth to make cream of tomato soup.)

● POULTRY

Make two herb bouquets of 1 bay leaf, 1 tablespoon tarragon, 1 teaspoon rosemary, 1 teaspoon thyme, and 1 tablespoon parsley. Cook the bird and bags in chicken soup ("boiled" chicken), and serve with one of the herb sauces.

● ● CHICKEN FRICASSEE WITH TARRAGON

Brown a quartered chicken which has been salted, peppered, and coated with flour in 3 tablespoons butter. Add 1 chopped onion and cook until the onion is tender. Transfer to a casserole. Rinse the pan with 3 cups chicken stock (or 2 cups stock and 1 cup dry white wine) and pour over chicken. Add the herb bouquet, cover and simmer for 30 minutes. Remove the bag, add ½ cup heavy cream to the gravy and garnish with minced tarragon. By varying the contents of the bouquet, you can change the taste of the dish. Use dill instead of tarragon and finish the gravy with sour cream instead of cream. Use sage, rosemary, dried lemon peel, and white wine with the broth.

● BEEF

Make two herb bouquets of 1 teaspoon peppercorns, 2 cloves, 1 broken bay leaf, 2 teaspoons each of thyme, marjoram, and savory, 1 tablespoon parsley, and ½ teaspoon crushed lovage.

● ● BRAISED BEEF

Season a rump or chuck roast (4-5 pounds) with salt and pepper, rub with flour, and sear in hot oil or fat.

Add a minced onion and carrot. Cook slowly for 10 minutes before adding herb bouquet, 2 cups tomato juice, ¼ cup orange juice, and ½ cup red wine. Bring to a boil, cover, and cook in a 325° oven for about 3 hours. Vary by using the basic bouquet, 3 large sliced onions, and substitute 1 cup beer and 2 cups broth for the liquid.

● FISH
The liquid used to cook shellfish or to poach whole fish, fillets, or steaks is called court bouillon. Make a herb bouquet with 1 bay leaf, 2 peppercorns, 1 teaspoon each of thyme, fennel weed, and lovage, and 1 tablespoon parsley.

●● COURT BOUILLON
Combine 3 tablespoons each of minced onion and carrot with the above herb bouquet. Add 2 cups stock (½ white wine or vermouth, ½ water; or water, wine, and clam juice). Simmer shellfish in this stock, cool, and remove to a dish. Serve with herb sauce. Poach a whole fish such as mackerel or salmon in court bouillon. Scrape off the skin and serve hot with fennel butter or cold with a herb mayonnaise or Hollandaise sauce.

●● FISH FILLETS
Cover 2 pounds fillets in a pan with court bouillon. Bring to a boil and simmer until the fish is barely done. Remove the fish to an ovenproof serving platter, reduce the remaining liquid to 1 cup and use it to make velouté sauce. Add ½ cup thick cream, spread sauce over fish, sprinkle with grated Swiss cheese, and brown under the broiler.

Rice

Rice constitutes the basic food of more than half the world's population. It is an amazingly versatile food if you are willing to spend just a little time and effort on it. A good beginning is to add ½ cup minced chives or 1 cup minced parsley to a dish of cooked, buttered rice.

☐ BASIC PILAF
In 2 tablespoons melted butter, sauté 1 tablespoon minced shallot or 1 small onion. Add 1½ cups raw rice and stir until the grains turn milky. Add salt, herbs, and 3 cups boiling liquid. Cover, and bake 25 minutes in a 375° oven (or turn the heat to low and cook for about 18 minutes on the top of the stove). The liquid depends on what the rice is to be served with. This usually means chicken stock, but you might also use beef stock or fish stock (water and clam juice).

● LEMON-DILL RICE
Add 1½ teaspoons dried lemon peel, 1 tablespoon dill weed, and 1 teaspoon chives.

● MIXED HERB RICE
Add 2 teaspoons each of savory and

COOKING WITH HERBS
Rice dishes
Risottos
Stuffings

---

marjoram, 2 tablespoons chervil and parsley; *or,* 2 teaspoons each of thyme, basil, and rosemary and 2 tablespoons parsley.

● BASIL RICE

Add 1 tablespoon finely minced basil and 2 tablespoons parsley. Substitute ½ cup tomato sauce for the same amount of stock.

● MEXICAN RICE

Sauté 1 minced clove of garlic with onion. When the rice is milky, add 2 tomatoes (1 cup canned), peeled, seeded, and chopped, and allow to cook until almost all the moisture is gone. Add chicken stock, 2 tablespoons minced mint leaves, and 1 cup fresh peas. Cover and bake. Sprinkle finished dish with finely minced coriander leaves or parsley.

● PAKISTANI RICE

Crack the following herbs and spices in a mortar and pestle or with a rolling pin and place in a 4-inch square piece of cheesecloth: 5 whole cloves, 5 coriander seeds, ¼ teaspoon cumin seeds, ¼ teaspoon peppercorns, 2 3-inch cinnamon sticks, and 2 bay leaves. Tie and add to the rice and stock. Add 1 pound peas cooked in butter to the finished rice, if desired. Toss the rice with 1 tablespoon lemon juice and garnish with ¼ cup minced parsley.

The addition of cooked meat or shellfish 10 minutes before the end of cooking time makes the pilaf into an economical and light lunch or dinner dish.

● PEPPERONE RISOTTO

Add 2 teaspoons rosemary as the herb, and sautéed pepperone sausage to the basic pilaf.

● CHICKEN LIVER RISOTTO

Cook ½ teaspoon dried, powdered sage with rice. Add sautéed chicken livers, kidneys, or sweetbreads, and garnish with 2 tablespoons finely chopped fresh sage. Sprinkle with Parmesan cheese.

● SHRIMP OR LOBSTER RISOTTO

Add ½ teaspoon each of mint and wild marjoram, ¼ teaspoon cumin seed, and substitute 2½ cups mixed clam juice and water and ½ cup tomato sauce for the broth. Add sautéed shrimp or lobster 10 minutes before serving.

Stuffings

Although sage is universally used in stuffing poultry, this strong herb has authority combined with pork, too. Use a sage stuffing to fill a crown roast or pockets slit in thick chops. This is one place where sage, rosemary and thyme do not overwhelm each other or the food they flavor.

□ PORK STUFFING

Add to bread crumbs 1 cup chopped celery, 1 onion, ½ teaspoon crushed fennel seeds, ½ pound washed cranberries, and ¼ cup undiluted orange-juice concentrate. Glaze with the rest of the orange juice and ½ cup honey. Use with a crown roast or a stuffed boned roast.

☐ POULTRY OR VEAL STUFFING

Add to the bread crumbs 2 tablespoons minced parsley, 2 teaspoons marjoram, 1 teaspoon thyme, 2 tablespoons minced shallot, a pinch of nutmeg, and 12 chopped oysters or ¼ cup chopped ham.

Breads

You have already experimented with herb butters *on* breads; it is also possible to add herbs to bread dough before baking.

☐ BASIC BISCUITS

Sift together into a bowl 2 cups flour, 2 teaspoons baking powder, and 1 teaspoon salt. With the tips of your fingers, combine 5 tablespoons butter cut into small pieces with the flour until the consistency is that of coarse meal. Add herbs (see below) and two-thirds cup milk or light cream. Roll out, cut, and bake at 425° for 15 minutes.

● HERB BISCUITS

Add 2 teaspoons dried finely crushed herbs. This might be marjoram or thyme. With rosemary, use only 1 teaspoon.

● CHEESE BISCUITS

Add ¼ cup Cheddar cheese, 1 teaspoon each of thyme and powdered sage; *or,* omit the herbs and sprinkle cheese biscuits with caraway seeds.

● DILL AND CHIVE BISCUITS

Use three-quarters cup sour cream in place of the butter. Add 2 tablespoons each of finely chopped chive and dill.

The basic recipe for yeast bread given below can be used to make two regular loaves, or the dough can be shaped into long French loaves on a cookie sheet. Make it into hamburger buns, or roll out, spread with butter and herbs, and roll up like a jelly roll. Use either all white flour, half white and half whole wheat, or rye flour and whole wheat. Add dry herbs crumbled between your palms with the dry ingredients; fresh minced herbs should be added during mixing.

☐ BASIC YEAST BREAD

Scatter 1 package or 1 tablespoon yeast and 1 tablespoon sugar on ¼ cup warm water and let stand for 5 minutes. Add three-quarters cup warm water, 1 cup warm milk, 3 tablespoons melted butter or oil (1 egg added at this point makes a finer-textured loaf). Stir in 2 cups flour and beat. Incorporate 2 or 3 cups of flour to make a workable dough. Place on a floured surface and knead until smooth and satiny (up to 10 minutes). Place dough in a buttered bowl and cover; allow to rise in a warm place until it doubles in bulk.

COOKING WITH HERBS
Herb breads
Limpa
Desserts

Punch down, shape into desired form, and let it rise again. Bake in 375° oven for 40 minutes for loaves, 20 minutes for buns.

● SAGE BREAD
Add 2 teaspoons dried, powdered sage and ½ teaspoon nutmeg.

● HERB MIXTURE
Add ¼ cup minced onion, 1 teaspoon each of rosemary and thyme; *or,* try 1 teaspoon each of marjoram, thyme, and summer savory.

● DILL BREAD
Substitute 2 cups creamed cottage cheese for the liquid, add the egg, ½ teaspoon baking soda, and 2 tablespoons minced dill weed. Stir the flour in until well mixed, but do not knead. When it has risen once, stir down and put in buttered casseroles or bread pans. Allow to double, and bake like basic yeast bread.

● CUMIN BREAD
Omit sugar and add 2 tablespoons honey. Substitute orange juice for half of the water, use half white and half whole wheat flour, and add 1 tablespoon crushed cumin seed.

□ LIMPA
Sprinkle 2 packages of yeast and one-third cup sugar over ½ cup warm water. Let stand 5 minutes and add 1 cup warm milk, ¼ cup molasses, 2 eggs, 2 tablespoons grated orange rind, 1 teaspoon salt, 2 tablespoons crushed anise and fennel seeds, 2 tablespoons soft butter and 2½ cups rye flour. Stir and add 2 to 3 cups of white flour. Knead until smooth. Place in buttered bowl and let rise. Punch down, shape into 2 roundish loaves on a cookie sheet dusted with cornmeal, let rise again and bake at 375° for 30-35 minutes.

Modern cookbooks suggest brushing breads, rolls, and pastries with an egg yolk beaten with 1 tablespoon water and sprinkled with poppy seed. Pliny, in the First Century A.D., first advocated this in his writings on herbs and foods. Try caraway, fennel, and sesame seeds as alternatives to poppy seed.

Desserts

Herb seeds are a most satisfactory aid to flavoring desserts. Add 1 tablespoon of fennel seed to apple or berry pie; ¼ cup toasted sesame seed to the crust of a chocolate pie, or substitute 1 cup toasted sesame seeds for the pecans in your pecan pie recipe; add 1 tablespoon of crushed coriander seed to gingerbread. Try anise syrup poured over fresh fruit desserts.

□ BASIC ANISE SYRUP
Make a syrup of 1 cup sugar, 1½ cups water, ¼ teaspoon aniseed, a dash of salt. Boil for 5 minutes. Use this to flavor all or any of these fresh fruits; orange and grapefruit sections, apples, grapes, pears, and pineapple.

Allow to mellow several hours in the refrigerator.

● PEAR COMPOTE
Poach fresh, halved pears in anise syrup until tender. Add ¼ cup brandy as they cool in the syrup, and serve with a scoop of coffee ice cream and some syrup in each bowl.

☐ RHUBARB AND ANGELICA PIE
Cut into 1-inch pieces enough rhubarb to make 3 cups and enough tender angelica stems to make 1 cup. Mix them with 1¼ cups sugar, 2 tablespoons flour, 1 tablespoon lemon juice, and a little salt. Put into 9-inch pie plate lined with pastry, cover with top crust, and bake for 10 minutes at 425°. Reduce heat to 350° and bake 25 minutes longer.

☐ SEED CAKE FOR TEA
Butter and flour an 8-inch layer cake pan or savarin pan. Cream 1 cup butter with 1½ cups sugar. Beat in 4 eggs and add sifted 2 cups flour, 2 teaspoons baking powder, ¼ teaspoon salt. Add herb seed and grated rind, pour in pan and bake at 375° for 45 minutes.

● SEED CAKE VARIATIONS
Add to cake batter 3 tablespoons caraway seed and ¼ teaspoon mace: *or,* 1 tablespoon crushed cumin seed, 1 teaspoon grated orange rind, and glaze with powdered sugar mixed with orange juice to spreading consistency; *or,* 1 tablespoon aniseed with a brandy glaze; *or,* 2 tablespoons dill seed and 1 teaspoon grated lemon peel with a lemon glaze.

Herb seeds are used to flavor cookies also. We have found it more effective to use a single flavor than to mix several in one recipe. Use this basic sugar cookie recipe and experiment to suit personal preference.

☐ BASIC HERB COOKIES
Cream 1 cup butter with 1½ cups sugar, add 2 eggs and 3 cups flour which has been sifted with 2 teaspoons baking powder and 1 teaspoon salt. Add herb seed (2 or 3 tablespoons crushed coriander seed; 2 tablespoons dill seed; 1 tablespoon aniseed; 1 tablespoon fennel seed), 2 teaspoons vanilla extract, and 1 teaspoon grated lemon rind. Refrigerate for at least 4 hours. Roll thin, cut into shapes, and bake on a greased cookie sheet about 10 minutes at 350°.

● SESAME BARS
Press sugar cookie dough into a greased 9" x 12" pan so that it is about an eighth of an inch thick. Cook 8-10 minutes. Remove from oven, and spread sesame seed topping evenly over dough. Bake for about 20 minutes or until done. Cool and cut into bars.

●● TOPPING
Bring to a boil in a saucepan 1 cup

COOKING WITH HERBS

Fig. 12. Decorative wreath of dried garden herbs. Photo by Oh Mama Photography.

butter, 1 cup brown sugar, 1 cup honey. Boil 5 minutes, remove from heat, stir in ¼ cup heavy cream and 1½ cups lightly toasted sesame seeds with a dash of salt. Very sweet.

□ SOFT CARAWAY COOKIES
Cream 1 cup butter with three-quarters cup sugar. Add 1 egg and 1 cup unsweetened applesauce. Sift 2 cups flour with 2 teaspoons baking powder and ½ teaspoon salt, and add to butter-sugar mixture with 1 tablespoon caraway seed and 1 teaspoon vanilla extract. Drop onto a greased cookie sheet and bake in a 375° oven. While they are still warm, frost the cookies with a glaze made with the juice of half a lemon, half an orange, the grated rinds, and enough powdered sugar to make it spread easily. For variety, try cumin seed instead of caraway.

Pickles, Candy and Jelly

Here are some ideas to add variety to your fare that are fun to try.

□ PICKLED NASTURTIUM BUDS
In a quart jar combine 1 tablespoon salt, 6 peppercorns, 2 cups wine vinegar, and 1 clove of garlic. Fill with green nasturtium pods, seal, and store a month before using. Use in place of capers.

When the colonial housewife served after-dinner mints, they were indeed that. But she also candied sage leaves, rose petals, clove pinks (gillyflowers), violets, borage blossoms, angelica and lovage stems. There are two methods for herb candy: the first, for candy to be used relatively soon; the second, for that which can be kept in airtight containers almost indefinitely.

□ CANDIED MINT LEAVES
(Or substitute fresh sage leaves, violet blossoms, borage, violas, or rose petals.) Select perfect leaves and blossoms. Wash and dry without bruising. Beat 1 egg white until it is frothy and paint onto the leaves with a fine paint brush. Sprinkle with granulated sugar, and dry thoroughly in a slightly warm oven with the door open. Store briefly between sheets of waxed paper.

□ CRYSTALLIZED BLOSSOMS
Select about 3 cups of blossoms removed from the stems. Cook 3 cups sugar in 2 cups of water to 238°, the soft crack stage. Pour into a shallow pan and place the flowers on a rack in the cooled syrup so that they float in it. Cover the pan with a wet towel to prevent crystallization at this stage and let stand 4 hours. Add more cooled syrup to cover and let stand overnight. In the morning lift out the rack and allow the flowers to drain and dry in the air. Store between sheets of waxed paper in an airtight container.

COOKING WITH HERBS
Jelly
Herb Vinegar
Herb Spices

☐ CANDIED ANGELICA STEMS
Use in Christmas fruitcake or with crystallized violets and borage blossoms to decorate a special cake. Cut stalks in July when the plant is in its second year. Cut into 3-inch lengths and peel off the tough outer skin. Soak overnight in water to which you have added 1 tablespoon each of salt and vinegar. Drain, cover with fresh water, and bring to a boil until the stems are green. Make a syrup of 1 cup water and 2 cups sugar, a touch of green food coloring, and cook until the stems look transparent. Place in jars, cover with syrup, and seal. Or dry thoroughly and store in an airtight container.

☐ BASIC HERB JELLY
Pour 1 cup boiling apple or crabapple juice on 2 tablespoons dried crushed herbs or ¼ to ½ cup fresh leaves and let stand for 20 minutes. Strain into deep saucepan and add 2 tablespoons cider vinegar or 1 tablespoon lemon juice and enough fruit juice to make 2 cups. Add 3 to 3½ cups sugar, bring to a boil, and stir in ½ cup bottled pectin. Boil hard 1 minute, remove from fire, pour into sterilized glasses, place a few leaves of the herb on top, and cover with paraffin. Try opal basil, fennel, rosemary, sage, mint and thyme. (This recipe makes three 8-ounce jars.) We like herb jelly on biscuits and with meats rather than on breakfast toast.

☐ HERB VINEGAR
Fill a quart jar three-quarters full of fresh leaves. Heat, but do not boil, good cider vinegar or red or white wine vinegar. Fill the jar to the top and seal. Mellow 3 to 4 weeks, strain, and use or bottle in smaller containers.

●Make basil vinegar using red wine vinegar.

●Opal basil imparts a beautiful red color to white wine or cider vinegar.

●Burnet or chervil in white wine or cider vinegar.

●Add 1 cup of sugar to mint vinegar.

●Use tarragon in white wine vinegar.

●Make a garlic vinegar with 12 garlic cloves and 1 teaspoon salt.

Herb Spices

☐ CURRY POWDER
In your mortar, powder together 4 tablespoons coriander, 1 teaspoon fennel, 2 tablespoons cumin, 1 tablespoon peppercorns, 1 tablespoon ground ginger, 3 tablespoons ground turmeric, and 1 tablespoon cayenne or red chili pepper for hot curry — or ½ teaspoon for milder curry.

☐ HERB SALT
Place a thin layer of uniodized salt on a cookie sheet, then a layer of herbs and another of salt. Leave in a 300° oven for 10 minutes. Break up the lumps of moisture and leave for

another 10 minutes. Check for drying, and when the leaves crumble
easily, powder the herbs with the
salt, add pepper and some paprika.
Make your own combination or try
this: an equal amount of thyme,
marjoram, chives, basil, parsley, wild
marjoram, half the amount of sage
and lovage, and 2 bay leaves for each
6 tablespoons of fresh herbs. You
may wish to mix this in your blender
briefly before putting in a container.
Use to sprinkle on salads, use in dips,
or — like other kitchen herb products
— to bottle distinctively and present
as a gift.

CHAPTER VIII

Herb By-products

Fragrances and perfumes ... Cosmetics ... Herbs for the bath ...
For the hair ... Potpourris ... Home dyeing ... Mordanting wool ...
Polishes and cleansers ... Candles ... Soap ... Bouquets ... Wreaths

HERB BY-PRODUCTS

CHAPTER VIII

The colonial homestead depended for its proper functioning on what the housewife could produce with the raw materials available to her. The kinds of herb products she assembled — room fresheners, cosmetics, dyes, bouquets, wreaths, and countless other household aids — can still be made at home today.

Fragrances and Perfumes

You can purchase real essential oils or try this simple method for capturing the oils of your own garden plants to use as perfume bases and bath oils, or in potpourris, scented candles, or soaps. Make only small amounts, since without expensive commercial fixatives to give them permanence, home fragrances are relatively short-lived.

☐ SCENTED OIL

Gather herb flowers and leaves and pack them loosely in a widemouthed jar. Fill this with some odorless oil (almond or sesame oil from a health food store, refined olive oil, or even melted lard) and let stand in a warm place for 24 hours. Strain through double cheesecloth. Then put a new herb harvest into the jar with the oil. Repeat this for a week or two until the oil has a strong odor. When that point is reached, strain or filter the scented oil into small, tightly capped bottles. This can be used as a perfume or bath oil, and in potpourris, scented candles and soap.

☐ PERFUME

Add strained scented oil to an equal amount of unscented *ethyl* alcohol from the drugstore. Do not use *isopropyl* alcohol which has an odor of its own. (Vodka can also be used, but because the proof is lower, is less effective.) Shake the mixture vigorously every day for a week. Allow the perfumed alcohol to separate from the oil and pour it off. The oil will be scented too, so save it. Or extract herb fragrances directly into alcohol by following the same process used for oil, substituting alcohol for the oil.

Herb fragrances can be used alone or in combination. Some herbs which make interesting scents are tarragon, bay, rosemary, mint, fennel seeds, thyme, basil, cumin, lavender, rose geraniums, lemon verbena, orange mint, peppermint, pennyroyal, and dried woodruff.

Toiletries

All herbal toiletries both commercial and homemade (colognes, aftershaves, after-bath lotions, and astringents) are essentially the same thing: scented alcohol to which an emollient, or softening agent, has been added. After-shave lotions and preparations for contracting or tightening the skin tissues are made with mildly astringent herbs such as sage, rosemary, burnet, agrimony, St. Johnswort, yarrow, rose petals, lady's mantle, and southernwood. Here are some simple recipes.

☐ COLOGNE
Add enough of your perfume to 1 cup ethyl alcohol to scent it pleasantly.

☐ AFTER-SHAVE LOTION
Use any of the herbs suggested and extract directly into ¾ cup alcohol. Add 1 teaspoon glycerine, purchased from the druggist, and ¼ cup cold water. (Or use plain ethyl alcohol and 1 tablespoon homemade perfume.) Experiment with lavender, peppermint, tarragon, and anise.

☐ ASTRINGENT
To contract or tighten the tissues of the skin. Put a small cucumber into your blender, rind and all. Strain the juice and to it add an equal amount of astringent herb extracted directly. For extra mildness, add an equal part of herb decoction.

☐ AFTER-BATH LOTION
With a whisk or a fork, mix 1 egg yolk with 1 tablespoon each of glycerine and oil. When thoroughly mixed, beat in 1 cup herbal extract (alcohol and 2 or more teaspoons herbal perfume).

Cosmetics

☐ MASK FACIAL
This will both cleanse and tighten the skin. Beat the white of an egg with 2 tablespoons very strong astringent herb decoction. Add 1 or 2 teaspoons homemade peppermint extract. Use the entire mixture for one facial or refrigerate.

☐ SKIN CREAM
Simmer covered 1 ounce comfrey or camomile in one-third cup water for 15 minutes. Strain. Into a small bowl put ½ cup oil and beat in 1 egg yolk. When entirely mixed, beat in the tea slowly. Use or refrigerate.

☐ MOISTURIZER
To soften the skin. Heat in a Pyrex bowl in a pan of simmering water 4 teaspoons beeswax (or white paraffin), 3 to 4 teaspoons lanolin, and one-third cup oil. Slowly add one-third cup very hot, strong camomile, rose petal, rose hip, or other herb tea and 2 teaspoons glycerine. Heat together for 5 minutes, remove from the boiling water bath, and beat at low speed with your mixer or a whisk. When the mixture is cool and as thick as mayonnaise, add some rose perfume oil and 2 teaspoons warm water. Continue to beat for a minute.

☐ FACIAL SAUNA
Make a blend of any of these herbs: rose petals, burnet, sage, lady's mantle, or yarrow. Put a handful of fresh herbs, or several tablespoons of dried, into a large bowl, and cover with enough boiling water to fill the bowl halfway. Cover your head with

HERB BY-PRODUCTS

Herbs for the bath
Herbs for the hair
Potpourris

---

a towel and hold your face over the bowl so that the steam trapped by the towel rises about it. Steam for 5 to 10 minutes, then pat on a herbal astringent.

Herbs for the Bath

Refreshing herbs for the bath are rosemary, lemon balm, mint, penny-royal, lavender, bay leaves, rose petals, wild marjoram, calendula, camomile, and comfrey. The last three are said to be particularly good for soothing the skin. Add 1 or 2 tablespoons of scented oil to the bath. Or simmer a handful of herbs in a quart of water for 10 minutes and let stand, covered, 20 minutes more before pouring this decoction into the bath water. Or, take a handful of herbs — singly or in combination — tie in a doubled cheesecloth or muslin bag, and add ½ cup oatmeal to make the skin particularly smooth. Hang this on the water tap while you are drawing the tub, let it float freely, or use as a washcloth.

Herbs for the Hair

The herb garden will also yield color tints, shampoos, and hair dyes.

☐ HAIR RINSE
For a blonde rinse, simmer 4 tablespoons camomile blossoms in a cup of water for 10 minutes. Brunettes can do the trick with 2 tablespoons crushed sage and 1 tablespoon dried rosemary (for a darker rinse, make the brunette decoction in an iron kettle). Pour the rinse through the hair several times or use with an equal amount of any mild shampoo.

● Rosemary and sage hair dyes are also safe for the lashes and brows. Just cover double-the-amount of herbs with water and simmer, covered, until a dark tint is reached (about 1 hour). Cool, dab on with cotton, and leave for an hour before rinsing with a little vinegar and water.

☐ HAIR-SET LOTION
Make a decoction of 2 tablespoons flaxseed, 4 tablespoons quince seed, and a drop of homemade perfume.

☐ SHAMPOO
Make a very strong rosemary decoction and add this to your own mild shampoo to combat dandruff. Or add a rosemary and sage decoction to 1 slightly beaten egg white. Massage this into your hair and scalp.

Potpourris

Yesterday's grandmothers made their room-fresheners by filling wide-mouthed crocks with alternating layers of salt and half-dried petals — roses, gillyflowers, and lavender being among the most popular. From this process comes the name potpourri (the French verb *pourrir* means to rot). Today, however, a simpler method preserves both the color and fragrance and can still be made in the home. It combines flowers and herbs with a fixative, spices, and essential oils. Fixatives make the scent of the mixture more lasting; the essential oils reinforce that aroma you wish to emphasize. Potpourris are usually made with a preponderance of rose petals and lavender, since these keep their fragrances well when dried.

Pick roses just as they are opening, when the sun is high and their volatile oils are most concentrated. Be sure they are perfectly dry. Remove the petals and spread them on a rack in an airy place. When dry, store the petals in a large screw-lidded glass container until the rest of the material is ready. Dried lavender blossoms can be separated from their stems by taking a handful and rubbing them across a coarse screening or hardware cloth. Other flowers will add color to your mixture but will not impart scent: beebalm, bachelor buttons, carnations, larkspur, delphinium, calendula and violets. Some herbs to use in your potpourri are thyme, rose-geranium leaves, lemon crispum geranium, lemon balm, costmary, lemon verbena, bay, and rosemary. Add some coriander or caraway seed and spices — cloves, nutmeg, cinnamon stick, allspice and mace. Other materials to have on hand before mixing the potpourri are dried citrus peel — from oranges,

lemons, and tangerines — and some essential oils like rosemary, lemon verbena, peppermint, bergamot (the last oil is made from oranges and can be purchased) and rose geranium.

Sweet woodruff is one of the few herbs with a built-in fixative. It contains coumarin, which helps the dried sweet leaves retain their scent. The only other fixative that could be grown in your garden is orris, a powder made from the root of the Florentine iris. However, this and other fixatives such as gum benzoin and storax are available from the druggist. The general rule to follow in making potpourris is to take a quart of dried petals and herbs and add ¼-½ cup fixative, 1 tablespoon spices, 1 tablespoon crushed herb seed, a few dried citrus peels, if desired, and 10-20 drops of essential oils.

To start you off, here are some recipes.

□ DRY POTPOURRI
To 1 cup dry rose petals, add 1 cup lavender, ½ cup each of marjoram leaves, orange-mint leaves, thyme, rosemary, 4 crushed bay leaves, 1 tablespoon crushed aniseed, ¼-½ cup orris-root powder, crushed orange and lemon peel.

□ MOIST POTPOURRI
Dry rose petals for 24 hours to make a quart. Layer petals and about 1 cup coarse or uniodized salt in a screw-lid

HERB BY-PRODUCTS

Potpourris
Home dyeing
Mordanting wool

jar. Make a combination to equal about 3 cups of lavender, rosemary and lemon-scented herbs, and place on top of the rose and salt mixture. Combine (1 teaspoon each) nutmeg, cinnamon, cloves, aniseed, coriander with ½ cup orris-root powder, and pour on top of the herbs. Sprinkle this with rose-scented oil and a few tablespoons of brandy. Cover tightly and store at least a month. To use as a room freshener, open the jar and stir up from the bottom. Keep the jar closed when not in use. If the mixture needs revitalizing, refresh it with brandy. It will last for years.

The number of variations is endless. In the days before commercial spray cans and wicks, these fresheners were to be found in every room in decorative or beribboned jars. Roses and sweet-scented herbs, with or without the fixative, were stuffed in pretty fabric bags and put in with the linens, laid in drawers, hung in closets, or tucked under the guestroom pillows.

Home Dyeing

Spinning, weaving, and dyeing were as much a part of the colonial homestead as were cooking and washing. Vegetable dyes were universally used until the late 1800s, when they were supplanted by chemical dyes. Plants grown for dyeing included bedstraw, bloodroot, anchusa, camomile, lily-of-the-valley, dock, yellow flag, calendula, wild marjoram, safflower, St. Johnswort, dyer's greenwood, Fuller's teasle, and soapwort for washing wool.

Many dye plants given different colors as a season progresses. For example, St. Johnswort dyes green in the spring, later yellow, and finally gold. As with commercial dye lots, home dyes will probably not produce exactly the same color twice. Care should therefore be taken to provide a plentiful supply for any dyeing project.

Iron kettles were often used for mixing dyes but tended to produce "sad" or grayed colors. Today we use enamel, stainless steel, or glass utensils. Wool is relatively easy to dye because animal fiber absorbs stain more readily than plant fibers like cotton and linen.

Mordanting Wool

Before wool is dyed it must be processed in a mordant, to fix the coloring. Alum and cream-of-tartar mordants produce soft colors and are safer to use than chemicals, which are hard on the wool. Alum can be bought from the druggist; chrome, tin, and iron chemicals — which can produce a greater variety of colors from the same plant material — can be ordered from botanical supply houses.

Chrome brings out the richness of yellows, sometimes making them gold; iron dulls colors and sometimes gives a greenish hue to yellow and gold; tin brightens, often garishly. Tin should be used sparingly because too much makes wool brittle.

□ ALUM MORDANT

For 1 pound of wool use 3 to 4 ounces of alum (potassium aluminum sulphate) and 1 ounce cream of tartar (potassium acid tartrate) in 4 gallons water. Heat the mordant in a large pot (enamel, glass, or stainless steel) until lukewarm. Add washed fleece, natural wool, or white wool tied in skeins. Increase the heat, and simmer for an hour. (To wash a wool fleece soak it overnight in very hot water. Then lift it out and bathe it in a weak solution of soap suds. Rinse in hot water.) Cool the wool a little, squeeze out excess moisture before entering it into the dye pot, or leave it in the mordant overnight.

Chrome (potassium dichromate), *tin* (stannous chloride) and *iron* (ferrous sulphite): Mix ½ to 1 ounce of the chemical to 4 gallons water. These chemicals can also be added to the dye pot a teaspoon at a time at the end of the dyeing process to alter the color that has been produced on alum-mordanted wool. To experiment with colors divide the prepared dye into four utensils, leaving the first plain and adding a little chrome to the second, tin to the third, and iron to the fourth. Put a small skein of alum-mordanted wool in each.

□ GENERAL DIRECTIONS FOR DYEING WOOL

Cover the plant material with cold water and let it soak overnight. Generally count on a peck (about 7 quarts) of chopped or crushed herb material or 8 ounces of chopped root to dye 1 pound of wool. Bring to a boil and simmer for the specific time recommended. When ready to dye, pour in enough warm water to cover 1 pound of wool (about 3 to 4 gallons), enter the wool into the dye pot, bring to a boil, and simmer to the desired color. This will take 30-60 minutes. The color will generally be better if the plant material is left in during the dyeing process, but you may strain it out if you prefer. Put the wool in a pan of hot water to rinse. Repeat until the rinse water is clear. Dry dyed wool in the shade.

Although many herbs will yield a dye, here are some of the traditionally successful and colorfast dye plants (fresh or dried) you can raise and use, with special cautionary notes.

Reds

□ BLOODROOT

(Learned from the Indians and mentioned by Cotton Mather in the early

HERB BY-PRODUCTS

Yellow and gold
Burnt orange
Green

17th Century.) Dig this plant in summer and use 8 ounces of chopped root with alum-mordanted wool. Boil 30 minutes. Enter the wool and simmer until the desired color is obtained.

☐ LADY'S BEDSTRAW
Treat like bloodroot but boil only 15 minutes before entering the wool. Watch carefully, for it is delicate and the color will cook away if boiled too long.

Alkanet (anchusa) root is used particularly for coloring cosmetics. The red coloring is soluble in alcohol or oil. Extract the plant soaking in alcohol and add to a water bath for dyeing. Safflower yields a water-soluble yellow which when washed away leaves a red, soluble only in alkali.

Yellow and Gold

☐ WELD
Pick the plant as it comes into flower for a good yellow and use alum-mordanted wool. Use chrome-mordanted wool for old gold and olive. Simmer the plant material 1 hour and enter the wool. Simmer another 1 hour.

☐ AGRIMONY
Crush the dried flowers which appear in the early summer and simmer 25 minutes to extract dye; then simmer the wool for 30 minutes. Alum-mordanted wool dyes buff; chrome, gold; alum-chrome-vinegar, khaki (dye alum-mordanted wool and without rinsing put it into a bath containing, one-sixth ounce chrome and 7 tablespoons vinegar to 4 gallons water).

☐ COREOPSIS
Mordant the wool in ½ ounce stannous chloride and ½ ounce cream of tartar to 4 gallons water. Simmer the bright yellow flower heads 30 minutes, enter wool, and simmer for another 30 minutes.

☐ CALENDULA
Flowers dye a clear yellow with an alum mordant; gold with chrome. The flowers of the garden marigold (*Tagetes* varieties) and the plant tops of St. Johnswort mordanted in alum will also give yellows.

Burnt Orange

☐ COREOPSIS
Use chrome as a mordant, and about twice the number of flowers as usual.

Green
The following plants will yield soft yellow greens or gray greens. To obtain a deep green or blue-green, dye with yellow and over-dye with woad.

☐ TANSY
Gather spring leaves before buds form. Use alum-mordanted wool.

□ SORREL
Pick in the spring and use alum.

□ ST. JOHNSWORT
Alum-mordanted wool will dye yellow-green when the plant tops are picked in August, gray-green if picked in July. Soak overnight and simmer 1 hour to extract the color, then 1 hour more with the wool.

□ LILY-OF-THE-VALLEY LEAVES
Gather in spring and soak overnight. Simmer 1 hour, enter wool, and simmer another hour. Try adding 1 teaspoon or more lime (slaked lime or calcium hydroxide) at the end of the dyeing process to get a brighter green.

Violet

□ WILD MARJORAM
The flowering tops with alum mordant are reputed to yield violet. We have only dyed with the dried material, which gives a soft tan. Perhaps wild marjoram grown in different soil and used fresh would indeed yield violet.

Blue

Woad, the famous skin dye used to turn the ancient Britons blue, can be grown in this country. Extraction of the dye on a small scale has proved difficult, but this recipe from a quarterly journal of weavers and dyers in England has been recommended and is said to work satisfactorily.

□ WOAD
Cover woad leaves with boiling water. Weight them down for ½ hour. Strain off the liquid and to it add a caustic potash solution (potassium hydroxide) and a dilute hydrochloric acid. (These chemicals are dangerous to use, so exercise extreme caution and work out of doors if possible.) Wool, boiled in this liquid, will yield a rich indigo blue. If the leaves are left weighted for a longer period of time, greens and browns will result.

We understand that parsley and chervil, hyssop, germander, ladies mantle, wormwood, southernwood, Fuller's teasle heads, larkspur, and huckleberries mixed with ashes and elecampane root will also yield interesting dyes.

There are endless other uses for herbs.

Polishes and Cleansers

Alkanet root, dissolved in linseed oil and mixed with turpentine, can be used to polish dark furniture. A lemon-balm rub will give it a sheen and keep cats from clawing upholstery. Fresh sorrel leaves rubbed on copper pots that have been immersed in hot water will shine them. And sorrel will reputedly remove ink spots and corrosion.

Candles

When making candles, put several

HERB BY-PRODUCTS

Soap
Bouquets
Wreaths

---

drops of homemade essential oil into the melted paraffin or extract the scent from fresh leaves by immersing them in melted wax until they give up their fragrance. Coat ready-made candles with scented wax by pouring the wax over them or by dipping them and hanging them free to harden.

Soap

To wash delicate silks and woolens, stir fresh leaves of soapwort in warm, soft water. This herb contains saponin, which creates a lather in water.

Smoking Herbs

Nicotine-free herbal tobaccos have been used for centuries. Rub dried herbs to a coarse powder before filling your pipe. The English make a mixture in which coltsfoot predominates. The rest is made up of betony, eyebright, rosemary, thyme, lavender, and camomile. Other smoking herbs are marjoram, sage, chervil, woodruff, and angelica.

Incense

Put ½ teaspoon of powdered herbs on a piece of lighted charcoal for an herbal incense.

Bouquets, Summer and Winter

Herbs are also used to decorate the house with long-lasting, fresh-cut bouquets. Some are showy (beebalm, calendula, and allium blossoms), but the majority are used more for texture and color. The artemisias, silver king especially, provide a good background foliage. Sage leaves and flowers, wild marjoram, whorls of horehound with their natural curves— all complement the showy beebalm or a summer bouquet of garden flowers.

In winter, dried herbs can provide color throughout the house. Some herbs that dry easily and naturally and last for more than a year if not exposed to direct sunlight are: safflower heads, blossoming wormwood and silver king, teasle heads, yarrow and tansy blossoms, baptisia seed pods, sage leaves and seed pods, allium blossoms, woad seed heads, sweet cicely seed heads, wild marjoram, horehound, agrimony, flowering mints, yellow feverfew, thistle, dill and fennel heads, lamb's ears, ambrosia, and St. Johnswort.

Wreaths

You can also make decorative herb wreaths. To a circle of wire, tie a base of wormwood, lamb's ears, and silver king artemisia when they are in blossom and still fresh enough to be supple. When this background is thick and full, place them on screening to dry in a dark, airy place and forget them until the rest of the herbs have flowered or gone to seed. Some autumn evening, assemble your dried-herb seed pods and flowers and tie them to the dried base with florist wire.

A Tussy-Mussy Nosegay

Fresh herbs can also be used imaginatively to make an old-fashioned tussy-mussy or Elizabethan nosegay. Originally these were hand-carried bouquets used to combat objectionable odors; later they became flowers with a message.

Dictionaries of the language of flowers were popular in the eighteenth and nineteenth centuries, when flowers served to express the thought and sentiment of the giver. But use discretion; even authorities give diverse meanings to each herb (see box), and your sentiment might be misinterpreted by a knowledgeable recipient.

To make a tussy-mussy you will need a small paper doily, ribbon, aluminum foil, or green waxed florist paper. Scented geranium leaves make a good outer border, put bunched herbs within, and a flower in the center.

Yarrow – war
Marigold – grief
Nasturtium – patriotism
Sage – wisdom and domestic virtue
Cumin – avarice
Sweet marjoram – happiness
Caraway – faithfulness
Borage – courage
Thyme – bravery
Hyssop – sacrifice
Wormwood – absence or bitterness
Camomile – humility
Lemon balm – sympathy
Basil – love or hate
Rue – sorrow and repentance
Lavender – distrust and cleanliness
Tansy – immortality
Coriander – hidden merit
Parsley – festivity
Rosemary – remembrance

Gifts

The utilitarian herb can be used in so many ways to make gifts, large and small, right down to a catnip mouse for your pet. What could be better than a potted herb for a shut-in or a friend in the hospital? Its presence will raise the spirits and perfume the air. And in time it can be planted outside where it will be a living reminder of both the sentiment and the friend.

CHAPTER IX

Herbs as Pesticides

HERBS AS PESTICIDES

CHAPTER IX

Centuries before our present ecological concern, early writers on herbs — using quaint woodcuts and even quainter combinations of observation, superstition, and myth — had recognized the virtues of herbs as common pesticides which were effective both in the garden and in the house.

While scientific research is only now probing the mysterious interactions of plants, gardeners have known for hundreds of years that companion planting works, that plants — particularly herbs — exude aromatic oils which can either repel or attract insects, and that herbs planted among vegetables aid growth and flavor.

In 1638 an English gardener, Gervase Markham, suggested that garlic, onions, and leeks could be used to draw moles from their tunnels and stun them. Colonial herbals noted that bunches of tansy, yarrow, rue, or hyssop were helpful in dispersing ants and houseflies; tradition said that a clump of tansy set near fruit trees, raspberries and other cane fruits would help reduce infestations of insects. The colonial housewife knew that sickly plants recovered if camomile, the plants' physician, was cultivated nearby and that somehow combinations like beans and savory, potatoes and horseradish, cabbage and mint planted in adjacent garden rows gave healthy, pest-free results.

She also knew some gardening *don'ts.* Separate basil and rue, isolate fennel. These herbs have detrimental effects on one another and sometimes on other plants nearby.

A Pest-Free Garden

Herbs and flowers have replaced our conventional garden fence as insurance against both insect and animal predators. And by accident and choice, we are now interplanting them among the vegetables just as the early settlers did.

During the first years we took up gardening as summer residents, we found ourselves faced with the need to produce as much as we could in a short growing season and a limited area. In the rush of late May planting, I was soon disregarding the careful winter blueprint that meticulously separated vegetables from herbs, and herbs from flowers. Without interrupting my frenzy to return to the house and consult the plan, I was soon seeding rows of herbs like sage, marjoram, basil, and thyme wherever and whenever I could. Marigolds, nasturtiums, and feverfew were transplanted to spaces left from the early harvest of vegetables or gaps in the original planting. Gradually we adapted this approach to gardening as our knowledge of companion planting grew and the space increased.

This method has reaped unex-

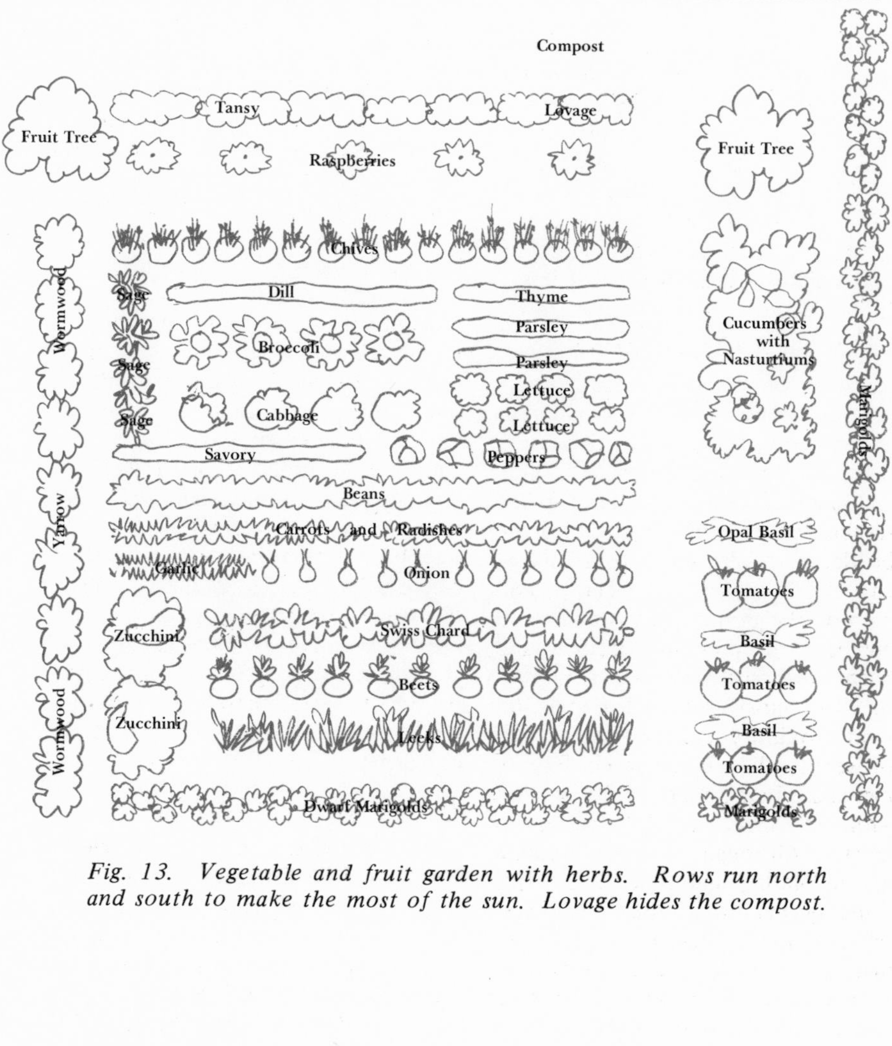

Fig. 13. Vegetable and fruit garden with herbs. Rows run north and south to make the most of the sun. Lovage hides the compost.

HERBS AS PESTICIDES

Onion family
Anti-nematodes
Tomatoes

---

pected results. The garden has become as free from pests as we could hope, although we still have our infections from time to time, and it looks better and is more inviting to work in. Inclusion of more of these helpful herbs has cancelled the use of sprays and dusts that would contaminate our food and might prove harmful to children.

The Allium, or Onion, Family

Some of the most easily grown perennials we find useful in this experiment are members of the allium family: onions, garlic, chives, and shallots. Planted adjacent to red raspberries, they deter the Japanese beetle. They also improve the flavor and health of nearby vegetables and help rid the garden of carrot flies and aphids that prey on lettuce and beans. Alliums are such a natural repellent most crops will benefit by their proximity and even the growth of weeds will be discouraged. Experiments are being conducted now with garlic-oil spray to kill mosquito larvae. Although in our climate onions, garlic, and shallots are customarily harvested when the stalks fall over and brown, they are perennials and can be left in the ground over winter. Chives, divided by separating their bulbous roots at least every three years, can rapidly be spaced out to form a permanent pesticide border.

Anti-Nematodes

African and French marigolds are another aid to plant health. These are not for the kitchen and should not be confused with pot marigold which was so essential to medieval and early colonial cooking. The oils secreted by the roots of the marigold are a natural enemy of the nematode, or selworm, which stunt the growth of tomatoes, eggplants, peppers, beans, and strawberries by feeding on their roots. However, at least two years is required for the soil to build up this secretion in order to be effective. Spaced among beans and cucumber hills, the odor of marigolds will repel the Mexican bean beetle and cucumber beetles. Being an annual, this plant will have to be sown each year, but it germinates quickly and thrives almost anywhere. Other plants said to discourage nematodes are calendula, scarlet sage, dahlias, and asparagus.

Tomatoes

Planted close to the asparagus bed, tomatoes will help rid the garden of the asparagus beetle. Basil and savory should also be interplanted with tomatoes because they will not only enhance the taste but also deter tomato worms and flies. Plantings of borage and mint are other deterrents to the tomato worm. Catnip fends off flea beetles.

Cabbage Health

Two common culinary herbs, sage and mint, should be planted among members of the cabbage family: broccoli, brussel sprouts, cauliflower, kohlrabi, and cabbage. They are used to combat cabbage moths, which can appear in white profusion throughout the garden. Other herbs for this purpose are rosemary, thyme, and dill. From my experience in weeding hyssop, I suspect its rank odor will also help deter this moth. If you plant a bed of mustard near the cabbage, the harlequin bug may be distracted from feeding on your vegetable crop.

The root maggot is another garden pest that will attack members of the cabbage family as well as turnips and rutabagas. Seeding radish among the rows will repel the maggot also and provide a quickly germinating row marker at the same time.

Insecticidal Herbs

Tansy, the old-fashioned perennial now coming back into favor, is a hearty, quickly spreading herb to use as an insecticide because of its strong, slightly medicinal odor. It will discourage the Japanese beetle as well as ants and flies.

Cut the hollow stems of angelica in short lengths if you can spare them from the kitchen uses and place them in the shady protection of other plants in the garden. They will attract earwigs, which you can dispose of by making a periodic collection early in the morning.

Plant the weedy-looking horseradish at the corners of the potato patch to fend off the Colorado potato beetle; it will also benefit tomatoes if they are nearby. Aphids are repelled by plantings of coriander and anise.

Members of the artemisia family are easily grown perennials with many insecticidal virtues. The fact that dogs avoid our wormwood plantings suggests that their natural oils may help reduce a wild animal invasion of the garden as well. We have alternated this herb with the equally pungent yarrow and a plant or two of horehound around the meadow perimeter of our garden and have not seen any recent evidence of breakthrough by rabbits, woodchucks, or deer.

Like southernwood, wormwood is a traditional moth repellent for the home. Others are yarrow, santolina, and lavender. I have found that southernwood or a few sprigs of pennyroyal placed in my hatband or rubbed on the backs of my hands and arms lessen the annoyance of blackflies and deerflies. Mint is also used for this purpose.

Planted with cucumbers and melons, the common nasturtium will attract black lice which might other-

HERBS AS PESTICIDES

Floral pesticides
Fenceless garden
Household uses

Fig. 14.   Cutting shears and tansy.
Photo by Stephen T. Whitney.

wise attack these plants. Other floral pesticides are coreopsis, cosmos, chrysanthemums, painted daisies, and feverfew.

Since we gave up commercial sprays and have depended on companion planting with herbs and flowers, beneficial insects have returned in greater numbers. These include the ladybug, praying mantis, and lacewing fly.

Though other factors, too, may have helped develop the effectiveness of our fenceless garden — variables such as insect cycles, temperature and moisture changes, and the build-up of organic matter in the soil through the continuing use of mulch and compost — it is clear, to this gardener at least, that herbs do play a great part in both controlling garden pests and increasing the yield and quality of our vegetables.

Household Uses

Indoors, supplies of fresh and dried herbs can also be used as pesticides to protect clothing and furniture, to discourage ants and fleas, and to dispel household odors.

Rue, the traditional herb used to prevent gaol fever, has been strewn or carried as a fumigant from early Roman times. Until fairly recently a bouquet of this bluish-green herb was always present to protect the judge when he sentenced a prisoner to death in the British courts.

117

Moth repellents
Pennyroyal for fleas
Anise for mice

Recipes for moth preventatives are so numerous in household-aid books, the forerunners of the modern cookbook, that this insect must have been of major concern. Some of the most effective herbs in dispelling this pest were tansy, wormwood, southernwood, lavender, peppermint, and curly mint. Pyrethrum, rosemary, and costmary were also dependable. The latter is sometimes called bible leaf, for the foliage was often used pressed as book marks by churchgoers and nibbled to revive the parishioners during the long Puritan sermons. All of these not only deterred moths but infused stored garments with pleasant outdoor odors.

The general rule for making your own moth preventative mixtures to hang in the closet or hide in bureau drawers is to add two tablespoonsful of spice, such as ground cloves, to four cups of bulk herbs.

For a sweet moth destroyer, try the following ingredients:
☐ Three-quarters cup each of dried rose geranium leaves, lemon balm, and lavender blossoms, one-third cup each of thyme, rosemary, and lemon verbena.
Or this:
☐ 1 handful each of crumbled thyme, tansy, and southernwood, 1 tablespoon powdered cloves, 2 handsful of lavender flowers and rosemary leaves, 1 tablespoon crushed cloves, and a generous sprinkling of dried lemon peels.

Use a handful each of dried santolina, tansy, mint, and wormwood; or try any of them by itself. Cut out and sew a 4-inch-square bag of cotton or percale and fill it with your mixture. Put them with your clothing and soon the odor will become pervasive.

Pennyroyal was used to rid the house of fleas, and some say it can be used as a cockroach deterrent by beleaguered city dwellers. It was also one of the strewing herbs, which were laid upon the floor and walked on — thus releasing the oils to purify the air and discourage insects. The burning of dried southernwood also purified the air.

Oil of anise is a mouse bait, and members of the mint family will drive mice away.

We still have much to learn about herbs as natural pesticides and the effects one plant has on another. Perhaps there is no more logical place than the home garden — with its necessary diversification — for modern man to study the mysterious and overwhelmingly beneficial interactions of these ancient plants with vegetables and flowers. At the same time we can help rid our houses of insects simply by harvesting and using what a bountiful Nature has provided.

APPENDIX A

Botanical Names of Major Herbs

It is important to be familiar with the botanical names of herbs. Regional names abound and some are often listed in seed-house catalogs. A list of Latin names is given here to avoid confusion and possible error. Medicinal herbs are termed *officinalis* ("from the apothecary shop") whether or not they are used as such today; herbs for dyeing are termed *tinctorius*; those for cultivation, *sativus;* and *oleraceus* is the botanical name given vegetables like cabbage, spinach, and purslane that were originally classified as herbs. Because herbal uses have become blurred with time, this nomenclature is often no longer distinctive.

Agrimony . . . . *Agrimonia eupatoria*
Angelica . . . . *Angelica archangelica*
Anise . . . . *Pimpinella anisum*
Basil . . . . *Ocimum basilicum,* sweet basil; *O. minimum,* bush basil; *O. crispum,* Italian; *O. purpureum,* opal basil
Bay . . . . *Laurus nobilis*
Bedstraw . . . . *Galium verum*
Beebalm . . . . *Monarda didyma*
Borage . . . . *Borago officinalis*
Burnet, Salad . . . . . *Sanguisorba minor*
Camomile, Roman . *Anthemis nobilis;* German, *Matricaria chamomilla*
Caraway . . . . *Carum carvi*
Catnip . . . . *Nepata cataria*
Chervil . . . . *Anthriscus cerefolium*
Chives . . . . *Allium schoenoprasum*
Comfrey . . . . *Symphytum officinalis*
Coriander . . . . *Coriandrum sativum*
Costmary . . . . *Chrysanthemum balsamita*
Cumin . . . . *Cuminum cyminum*

Dill . . . . *Anethum graveolens*
Dyer's Woad . . . . . *Isatis tinctoria*
Elecampane . . . . . *Inula helenium*
Fennel, Common . . *Foeniculum vulgare;* Florence, *F. vulgare* var. *dulce*
Feverfew . . . . *Chrysanthemum parthenium;* golden, *C. matricaria*
Horehound . . . . . *Marrubium vulgare*
Hyssop . . . . *Hyssopus officinalis*
False Indigo . . . . . *Baptisia tinctoria*
Lady's Mantle . . . . *Alchemilla vulgaris*
Lamb's Ears . . . . . *Stachys olympica*
Lavender, English . . *Lavandula vera*
Lemon Balm . . . . . *Melissa officinalis*
Lovage . . . . *Levisticum officinale*
Marjoram, Sweet . . *Majorana hortensis;* wild, *Origanum vulgare*
Mint . . . . *Mentha;* pennyroyal . . . *M. pulegium;* peppermint . . . *M. piperita;* spearmint . . . *M. spicata;* wooly applemint . . . *M. rotundifolia;* orange mint . . . *M. citrata*
Oregano . . . . see Marjoram (wild)

Parsley . . . . curly, *Petroselinum hortense* var. *crispum;* plain, *P. h.* var. *filicinum*
Pot Marigold . . . . . *Calendula officinalis*
Rosemary . . . . *Rosemarinus officinalis*
Rue . . . . *Ruta graveolens*
Sage, Common . . . . *Salvia officinalis*
St. Johnswort . . . . . *Hypericum perforatum*
Santolina . . . . grey, *Santolina chamaecyparissus; S. verdis,* green
Savory . . . . summer, *Satureia hortensis;* winter, *S. montana*
Sesame . . . . *Sesamum indicum*

Soapwort . . . . *Saponaria officinalis*
Sorrel, French . . . . *Rumex scutatus*
Southernwood . . . . *Artemisia abrotanum*
Sweet Cicely . . . . . *Myrrhis odorata*
Tansy . . . . *Tanacetum vulgare*
Tarragon . . . . French, *Artemisia dracunculus*
Teasel . . . . *Dipsacus fullonum*
Thyme . . . . English, *Thymus vulgaris;* Lemon, *T. citriodorus*
Weld. . . . . *Reseda luteola*
Woodruff, Sweet . . *Asperula odorata*
Wormwood . . . . . . *Artemisia absinthium*
Yarrow . . . . *Achillea millefolium*

APPENDIX B

Bibliography

For additional herbal information, consult The Herb Society of America, 300 Massachusetts Ave., Boston, Mass. 02115 or the following books.

Adrosko, Rita J., *Natural Dyes and Home Dyeing* (Dover Press)

Claiborne, Craig, *Cooking with Herbs and Spices* (Harper, Row)

Clarkson, Rosetta E., *Herbs — Their Culture and Uses* (MacMillan Co.)

Foster, Gertrude B., *Herbs for Every Garden* (E. P. Dutton)

Fox, Helen M., *Gardening with Herbs for Flavor and Fragrance* (MacMillan Co.)

Grieve, Mrs. M., *A Modern Herbal,* 2 vol. (Dover Press)

Leighton, Ann, *Early American Gardens* (Houghton, Mifflin Co.)

Lucas, Richard, *Common and Uncommon Uses of Herbs for Healthful Living* (Arco)

Mazza, Irma G., *Herbs for the Kitchen* (Little, Brown)

Meyer, Clarence and Joseph E., *The Herbalist*

Brooklyn Botanic Garden Pamphlets: *Handbook on Herbs & Dye Plants and Dyeing*

APPENDIX C

Sources for Herb Seeds and Plants

There are many herb sources included in the *Herb Buyers Guide,* published by The Herb Society of America, 300 Massachusetts Ave., Boston, Mass. 02115 (10¢).

Here are just a few:

W. Atlee Burpee Co., P.O. Box 6929, Philadelphia, Pa. 19132

Capriland, Silver St., Coventry, Conn. 06238

Greene Herb Gardens, Greene, R.I. 02827

Gurney Seed and Nursery, Yankton, S.D. 57078

Herb Cottage, Washington Cathedral, Mt. St. Alban, Washington, D.C. 20016

Meadowbrook Herb Nursery, Wyoming, R.I. 02898

Merry Gardens, Camden, Me. 04843

Nichols Garden Nursery, 1190 No. Pacific Hwy., Albany, Ore. 97321

Oak Ridge Herb Farm, RD 1, Box 461, Alton, Ill. 62002

Geo. Park Seed Co., Greenwood, S.C. 29646

Pine Hills Herb Farm, Box 307, Roswell, Ga. 30075

Otto Richter & Sons, Ltd., Locust Hill, Ontario, Canada

Snow Line Herb Farm, 11846 Fremont St., Yucaipa, Cal. 92399

Sunnybrook Farm Nursery, 9448 Mayfield Rd., Chesterland, Oh. 44026

Taylor's Garden, 2649 Stingle Ave., Rosemead, Cal. 91770

Tool Shed Herb Farm, Purdy's Station, N.Y. 10578

Waynefield Herbs, 837 Cosgrove St., Port Townsend, Wash. 98368

Herb Products

Aphrodisia, 28 Carmine St., N.Y., N.Y. 10014

Lhasa Kornak Herb Co., 2482 Telegraph Ave., Berkeley, Cal. 94704

Northwestern Processing Co., 217 N. Broadway, Milwaukee, Wis. 53202

Penn Herb Co., 603 N. 2nd St., Philadelphia, Pa. 19123

World-Wide Herbs, Ltd., 11 St. Catherine St. East, Montreal 129, Canada

A GARDENER'S JOURNAL

You will probably need a lot more room than these pages provide – I use a regular lined notebook for my records. But these four pages will help you start out right – keeping the record straight.

I. SEEDS AND PLANTS PURCHASED

Herb	Botanical Name	Annual Biennial Perennial	Source (where purchased)	Date	Amount	Cost

A GARDENER'S JOURNAL

II. CURRENT GARDEN PLANS (see diagrams, pp. 35, 36, and 40)

A GARDENER'S JOURNAL

III. PLANTING INFORMATION

Herb	Date Planted	Germination Date	Location	Remarks

A GARDENER'S JOURNAL

Experience is a great teacher. Next year's garden will profit from the recorded successes, disappointments, and discoveries of this year's.

IV. NOTES FOR NEXT YEAR'S GARDEN